Beyond Compassion

A Story Of
The Love That
Took Them Home

Cathryn Taylor

ISBN-13: 978-1977635938
ISBN-10: 1977635938

Many of you feel grief in response to your loss of a vital relationship, or your security due to the loss of your homes, or livelihood. Some of you may even be experiencing a decrease in your self-esteem in response to these losses which can eventually lead to a loss of your faith.

This book is about loss. The story speaks of the loss of loved ones, but the methods used to cope with those losses apply to any loss which may come your way.

In today's world, these methods can be especially relevant.

"Beyond Compassion" invites you to see the opportunity for change and transformation offered through loss. You will be introduced to methods which can be easily applied to any grief–methods that empower you to become a "student" of your loss as opposed to a "victim" of it.

Love to all who have the courage to grieve…

PRINTED BOOKS BY CATHRYN

(Also available as eBooks with linked audios and videos on Cathryn's website)

Cathryn's bestselling _The Inner Child Workbook_

(Available at Barnes and Noble, Borders and amazon.com)

Life Beyond Confusion And Fear

…an overview of the three stages of addiction and recovery…

MAXIMIZED

…a shamanic tale about a road trip with her dog named Max…

Which Lifetime Is This Anyway?

… a metaphysical bible for multidimensional healing…

SOUL STEPS

…an innovative 90-day Program integrating body, mind, heart and Soul...

(Available through www.iuniverse.com or call 1.800.authors)

EBOOKS BY CATHRYN

SHARE THE GIFT SERIES - _introducing signature "Interactive Tapping"_

As applied to:

Attracting Intimate Relationships;

Attracting Abundance;

Attracting Right Livelihood and

Developing Reciprocal Partnerships with Inner Child Work and EFT

Accept Who You Are- Get What You Want!

… A five step program that takes you into self-acceptance and depicts the connection between t his and your attracting all that you desire. Includes a 30-day EFT/Inner Child video program!

(All books are available through Cathryn's website.)

Please feel free to visit at www.EFTForYourInnerchld.com

Dedication

This story is dedicated to Gregg Braden.
His words reached into the depths of my heart and
magnified the courage needed to follow the path I had charted.

It was the last weekend that Kelly, my canine friend of thirteen years, and I had together. She was sick. It was time to let her go. We were visiting my Mother in Nebraska. That following Monday, Kelly and I would be taking our last road trip through the back roads of the Midwest returning to our home in Minnesota. The Vet was scheduled to assist us in Kelly's transition a few hours after we returned.

But on this wintry afternoon, I was frozen in fear. That inevitable stench of grief had once again seized my belly.

I put in Gregg's video, *"Walking Between The Worlds."* I kept hearing his words, "I had an opportunity." About loss and challenges, I kept hearing him use these words.

His examples became my companion on the last leg of this journey. Every tear fell on my cheeks with the knowledge its release was altering the electrical charge of my attachment. I knew my heart had been cleared. I had achieved compassion in this situation. I was anxious to see what came next.

However, I had no idea this experience was merely the dress rehearsal for what I would be experiencing with my own Mother just six, short months later. But that was the case.

BEYOND COMPASSION is a testament to that journey.
It is a celebration of the triumph achieved.
Gregg Braden was an invaluable guide.
For this, I will always be grateful.
Bless you, Gregg, and thank you.

Note to you the reader...

In the closing scene of the movie, GHOST, the character, Sam, played by the late Patrick Swayze, says, "Molly, it's beautiful. You get to take the love with you." And then he walks into the Light.

I believe the same is true for those of us left behind.

Love is the connector.

Love transcends loss.

Love is the emotion which defies boundaries and bridges the physical and spiritual worlds.

Love is energy. It encompasses those who love in a protective bubble.

It is a force field which does not die. The body dies, but the spiritual connection does not. It lives on and continues to protect, nurture and enhance.

This is a story about the transformative powers of that force field of love. It is about the change our heart can experience when we have the tools to stay open to that love and breathe through the gut-wrenching feelings of loss.

I invite you, now, to grab a cup of coffee or tea on a lazy afternoon and take the time to remember. Remember the love. Breathe it in. Close your eyes. Then take a stroll down the path lined with your own losses. Use the tools I provide and chart your own course to bliss, joy and a never-ending connection to those you love.

Cathryn Taylor
October 18, 2009
St. Paul, Nebraska

Contents

The Dress Rehearsal

Chapter One:
THE BEGINNING

The following is a story of how the loss of my pet became the dress rehearsal for the ultimate loss of my Mother. It is a story about how those very losses opened doors to my heart, and my faith that I did not even know had closed.

When I first realized it was time to help Kelly, my canine friend of thirteen years, release from her body and transition into the spirit world, I had no idea that that very experience would prepare me for the same journey I would, just short, six months later, travel with my own Mom.

But as you will see it did exactly that.

Therefore, before you can fully value the profound experience I had with Mom during her last six months on the planet, it is necessary to hear the story of how the decisions made in the last five weeks of Kelly's life prepared the way. I cannot tell you how many times I drew strength from experience with Kelly when confronting the myriad of feelings which emerged when faced with the same transition for Mom.

The story actually begins in October of 2008. I had just returned from one of the richest experiences of my life. My niece and her fiancé had asked me to perform the marital ceremony for them in Palm Springs. The wedding was a grand affair. I was so humbly honored to be asked to officiate it.

I marveled at how precisely Michelle and Ryan had selected every aspect for their wedding. Each detail, each invitation, each and every candle had been hand-picked.

The ceremony was no different. The three of us had worked very mindfully on the exact wording and phrasing.

The fear was that, as Michelle's Aunt, I would become so overwhelmed with emotion and sentiment I would be unable to pull it off without uncontrollable tears.

But that was not the case.

Something happened when the three of us met for our meditation and prayer. A synergy was established – a force field constructed that set the stage for a very high energy to emerge.

Consequently, the ceremony was delivered without a hitch. Many commented afterward that it was the best wedding they had ever attended. My own brother was so impressed that, even before the wedding party had fully exited, he had called Mom to tell her how proud he was of me.

She, unfortunately, was unable to attend the event. It was one of the heartaches of her later years.

It was definitely a milestone in my spiritual attainment.

I had conducted many ceremonies in my career and while on my path – but never before had my family members witnessed this part of me so intimately. It was an initiation of some sort – a coming out if you will.

I returned home with a new conviction, a new reverence for the choices my spiritual path had charted. It was just one week later that I had to make one of the biggest choices of my life.

CHAPTER TWO:
THE REALIZATION

Kelly had known before I did it was time. She knew there was something wrong with her body.

It was confirmed there was a growth near her heart. My spiritual teacher tuned into her. *"She wants to go home. She doesn't want to suffer, and she doesn't want you to suffer."*

Acceptance of this fact seeped slowly into my consciousness. A hollow feeling invaded my belly, that feeling which takes hold of one's stomach when it confronts loss. Kelly and I had walked this earth together for over thirteen years. She had been my traveling companion through one of the biggest choices of my life made just twelve years earlier.

After living in the San Francisco Bay area for over twenty-seven years, I moved to Minneapolis, Minnesota to unite with my husband and his three children. Kelly had accompanied me through the climate change, the culture shock and the adjustment from one lifestyle to another. One week later I was faced with the realization that it was time to assist my beloved canine friend in her transition to the other side. My thoughts raced – to memories – through fears – to possibilities. And now, just one week after this spiritual feat, I was to face it was time to assist my beloved Kelly in her transition to the other side.

I knew I was going to need all the conviction I could muster to accomplish the task that was before us. She had gone everywhere with me. She greeted me in the morning with her wagging tail and followed me around the house as if my every step were an adventure. She looked at me with those heartfelt eyes whenever I had the audacity to leave the house without her.

Inevitably, unless the weather were prohibitive, I would grab her leash, and we would be on our way. Once in the car, she would sing with the wind. When she tired of that she would come up behind me and burrow her head into my collarbone as if she were giving me a great big hug.

Yes, Kelly was definitely one of a kind.

Trying to imagine life without her was difficult. Staying open became the challenge. Neutralizing the fear became the antidote. The only thing that saved me was an energy therapy technique called tapping. I had learned that stimulating specific meridian points on the body with a gentle tap sent an electrical current which neutralized whatever emotion or symptom was being experienced at the time.

The technique is actually a self-administered form of acupressure. Gary Craig, an engineer out of California, had popularized a version of tapping called *emotional freedom techniques*. I had been trained in its application and had integrated tapping into my work and even into my day-to-day life as a way to cope. Whenever I confronted a challenging situation, I would tap away as I neutralized the feelings and allowed myself to return to a state of grace and peace.

But this situation took this practice to a brand new level. I didn't just neutralize feelings at the moment. I had to continually neutralize the steady flow of a variety of triggered emotions from my past. They hit the shores of my consciousness with the surge of the evening tide.

Every aspect within me who felt attached to Kelly, who had shared her life with Kelly, was given a chance to say her good-byes. The situation triggered residual losses as well. Every polyp of unattended grief reared its ugly head demanding resolution.

The situation was not urgent. We had time. I grieved. The children within me grieved. And Kelly and I began the journey of preparation.

One day, in the midst of tending to this process an opportunity presented itself. With that opportunity, came a shift.

CHAPTER THREE:
THE OPPORTUNITY

It occurred when I was running at the gym. I often use my workout time to process material that is lingering in my psyche. On this particular morning, I began to envision what it would be like at that precise moment when we assisted Kelly in going to the other side. The "mind movie" which emerged took my breath away.

In my mind's eye, I saw my husband, the Vet and me all gathered around Kelly. Her head was resting on my lap. All was peaceful. The song "Somewhere in Time" was playing in the background. Lights were low. Candles from Michelle and Ryan's wedding were burning. There was softness in the air. The reverent mood had been set.

At the precise moment Kelly's spirit left her body, it spiraled right into the center of my heart cascading my entire being with compassion and unconditional love. I cannot even begin to describe the feeling I experienced. It mimicked a soul transfusion.

I realized or was told by my inner teachers, that the vibrational frequency of my heart had, at that very moment, been elevated. I watched as the force field which dissolves the separation between spirit and matter took form around me.

My higher teachers went on to explain there did not have to be a loss. Kelly's transition could be a portal of entry for me to experience a union beyond my imagination. "Because of the closeness you and your pet experience you have the opportunity, literally, if you chose to do so, to experience the transition with her while staying in the density of your physical form. You can come to know what it is like to be of both worlds, where there is no separation, no here or there. With a switch in your consciousness scale, a line to each other can be forever forged, a force field created, that never dies. You truly are one. There does not have to be a separation. There is no such thing as death."

I could barely finish my run. "What a concept," I thought. "Could this really be or is this simply my feeble attempt to avert dealing with this loss head on?"

At that time I didn't know. I didn't know for sure what would transpire on the actual day of Kelly's release. What I did know was that Kelly and I had almost a month to prepare.

WHAT KEEPS US
FROM ENGAGING
IN THE EXPERIENCE OF LOSS?
THE FEAR WE WILL NOT SURVIVE!
THE FEAR
WE WILL NOT BE ABLE TO COPE
WITH THE INEVITABLE LOSS
OF THAT LOVE!
SO WE AVOID;
WE HOLD BACK.
WE DENY OURSELVES
AND OTHERS
OF THE EXPANSIVE EXPERIENCE
WHICH CAN BE FOUND
JUST AROUND THE CORNER
OF OUR FEAR!

CHAPTER FOUR:
WHAT IF I CAN'T COPE?

A few days later I had another moment of enlightenment, but there are several key events which, I believe, led up to the following experience.

The first came while I was being interviewed on a radio show. One of the statements I was surprised to hear myself say was, *"What we most fear is that we will not be able to cope."*

That statement, although not new to me, rang in my ears for hours after the show ended. It felt relevant to this current situation because it inspired me to go more deeply into the parts of me who were afraid they would not be able to cope with the loss of Kelly.

It triggered feelings from my last experience when I was faced with the same situation with my dog called Max. I remembered how difficult his transition had been for me. It had taken me months to regroup. The experience was rich – but very painful.

However, from the moment I realized the time had come for Kelly to go, I sensed our experience was going to be quite different.

The circumstances were different, granted. But the entire climate was markedly different as well. Nonetheless, the knee-jerk reaction to this situation was indeed gut-wrenching.

So even though I knew I did not want to go through the incredible loss, in the same way, I went through it when I lost Max, I was haunted by the feeling that this response to loss could not be avoided? Was that not the price we paid for loving others so deeply, the dread of that unbearable grief when and if they have to leave?

As recent as a month earlier I had made the remark to a friend that anytime I was away from Kelly or had to leave her home I experienced this hollowness in the pit of my belly. I added with a smile, *"That can't be good. Boy, do I dread the moment I have to let her go."*

No, it is not as if I have had this cavalier relationship with Kelly. We have had a very *tied-to-the-hip* relationship. I let her into my heart in the same way I had let Max into it. But it had been fourteen years since Max, and I had said our good-byes.

On September 29th of 1994, I had assisted Max in his transition when I had helped release his spirit by putting his body to sleep on my father's grave. But that was then. Our story was shared in my book entitled, *MAXIMIZED*. I was acutely aware of the fact I was no longer that person. I knew my need to hold on had diminished, and my capacity to let go had expanded.

Yes, I had had many wonderful animal experiences since Max's transition. Most were with Kelly. But there were also significant exchanges between me and members of another species.

CHAPTER FIVE:
THE INSPIRATION

One experience, in particular, needs to be shared here because I realize that the true inspiration, or rather invitation, to *seize the opportunity* to experience Kelly's transition as an expansion rather than a loss really needs to be credited to another pet of mine, a love bird named Macillius.

For the past nine years, my husband and I have had love birds. About four years ago I woke up in the morning to find one of the love birds dead. I was heart-broken for the remaining love bird. I assumed he felt devastated and wanted me to respond to his loss by getting him another partner.

I began to notice, however, that at certain times in the day I would hear him chirping in the same quiet tone he used to chirp in with her. And he would be looking over his shoulder as if he were conversing with someone to the left of him just as he had done when Isis had been alive.

I observed this for quite some time.

I had heard that animals, who are pure spirit, do not know the difference between life and death because they are not attached to the physical plane. They are therefore free to relate to each other in spirit form. It occurred to me that perhaps this was the reason Macillius did not track that Isis was not really perched right by his side.

It was touching to entertain the thought that they indeed were still together. However, the grander significance did not resonate until I connected that memory to the experience I had had that day at the gym. It dawned on me that Kelly and I could perhaps experience the same connectedness Macillius and Isis had shown me.

I played with that possibility for several days.

One morning I was just sitting on the couch talking to Kelly and all of a sudden I turned to her and said, *"Maybe we don't have to wait until the Vet comes to experience the expansion into oneness. Maybe all we have to do is tune our hearts into each other and experiment with feeling that vibration of oneness now, today, while you are still in body, while we are still together in the physical plane. Maybe, if we can practice doing this now, then when the actual time comes to release your spirit by putting your body to sleep we will have already established our relationship to each other in these other dimensions."*

As I said this, my heart began this subtle, slow progression of expansion which encompassed the essence of Kelly and me. Like an inverted pyramid, the image allowed our respective vibrations to merge into one another and into *"all that is."*

At that precise second Kelly buried her head into my chest and cuddled up to me. No kidding. That really happened!

CHAPTER SIX:
THE INVITATION

As I cherished that moment, the inspiration came to share this experience. I realized maybe our experience could inspire others to tune into their own losses and heal their own grief. "Maybe," I thought, "Our story could help pets, and their owners transcend their separation from one another as well."

I have witnessed that many of us allow our hearts to open to pets in ways we do not let them open to our human companions. "Maybe," I thought, "These relationships can be the portal of entry into a new level of consciousness where there no separation, no loss. Instead, perhaps there can be an elevation of a consciousness which transcends the physical dimension. And in this very expansion, a never-ending connection can exist."

I began to realize it was this same frequency of compassion, acceptance, and trust we needed to access when we pictured our heart's desires. It became clear to me that if I could hold my intentions with this same oneness as I held this compassionate, all-encompassing connection I had for my beloved pet that I could truly embrace that which I was trying to attract? It was all energy – a vibration that attracted like vibrations.

Wasn't that what all of the experts were saying? To attract our desires, we had to be able to feel connected to those desires as if we were already one with them? We do not simply *attract* abundance, right livelihood, intimate relationships, perfect health or anything else. From this point of reference, *we become our abundance, right livelihood, intimate relationships and immaculate health, all that is. We merge with that force field and therefore attract it.*

CHAPTER SEVEN:
OUR LAST MISSION REVEALED

At that moment our last mission together was revealed.

I realized one of the true gifts of this journey with Kelly was that, until that time I had not had a point of reference for what really "being in the moment" meant. I had spoken those words. I had tried to imagine them. But I had no *point of reference* for so passionately wanting to stay connected to anything–be it person, place or thing.

Most often, when I had the opportunity to experience that depth of desire, it was so quickly followed by the gripping fear that I would fail that seldom did I allow that feeling to exist.

The fear of its loss and my inability to cope with that loss was too engulfing.

But that was before I had mastered the "art of coping" available through my exposure of and mastery of the technique called "energy tapping."

I began to comprehend that when I touched on those feelings of oneness inspired by my love for Kelly, and used the sequences of energy tapping to neutralize and move beyond the fear I would not cope, that I somehow moved into the grid of unconditional love where there WAS no fear of loss, no fear of failure, in fact, no fear at all. There was just a gentle, compassionate knowingness. This possibility of staying connected to Kelly through this process ignited my desire to confront anything within me that would stand my way. Never before had I experienced such conviction.

From *that* reference point, I not only felt a deep connection between Kelly and me, I also felt a new level of oneness with all of my desires.

CHAPTER EIGHT:
THE COURAGE AND PERSEVERANCE TO DO THE WORK

I became impassioned about this endeavor. Every morning Kelly and I rehearsed going to the grid together. I would sit down near her and go into meditation. I would envision our force fields merging and then connecting into the grid of unconditional love. Once there, I worked on expanding my heart. Having been trained in how to "access" the Akashic Records I called on their wisdom as well. They became my form of prayer. The Akashic Records are basically the records of the experiences of our soul from the beginning of its conception. They are also referred to in the Bible as one's *Book of Life*. I was taught to access them through the use of a sacred prayer. I also learned how to open the records of the soul of a relationship.

For the past seven years, since my friend, and Master of the Akashic Records, Dahna Fox, had taught me the prayer, I had often used this method to connect with the higher realms. I incorporate this into my day-to-day life and my work with others just as I do tapping sequences.

Every day I tuned into the divine light and opened the records of both Kelly and me – our respective records as well as the records of the soul of our relationship. It was within this energy of the Akasha that I would do our inner work. Kelly simply sat by my side lending her support as I tapped on any obstacle which appeared to be blocking our ability to sustain the energy of the light.

I worked with the parts within me who felt scared and alone. I identified their pain then neutralized it with the tapping sequences. I also did what is referred to as "surrogate tapping." It is tapping on behalf of another. I tapped to neutralize not only Kelly's physical pain–but also her fears about the actual procedure as well. I was tapping like crazy and persistently calming the fears within Kelly and me. I was committed to building the force field of illumination which would be needed to escort Kelly's spirit to that plane from which her next experience would begin.

I had my support system as well. My friend Kim and I got together, and she led me in a series of "pre-grief" sequences. She and I often got together for all-nighters and led each other through sequences which addressed our respective ailments. The pre-grieving I did prepared my inner children for the loss they were about to feel so that when the actual time came I, as the adult, was able to remain more present.

This experience proved to be incredibly valuable when I was faced with the loss of Mom. It equipped me with a formula for moving through the myriad of feelings of loss. I had learned to trust myself enough to know I could cope with the loss which made it safe to fully engage in the love and attachment so prevalent in the last few months Mom and I spent together. Had it not been for this experience with Kelly I am not sure I would have been as open-hearted with Mom for fear it would hurt too much when she did have to go.

RIDING THE WAVES OF FEAR
ABOUT LOSING KELLY
AND MOVING THROUGH
THE STAGES OF GRIEF
AND THE KNEE-JERK REACTIONS
OF WANTING TO
PULL AWAY AND SHUT DOWN
BECAME THE CONTRACTIONS -
THE LABOR PAINS
WHICH GAVE BIRTH
TO MY RESTORED FAITH
I COULD COPE
AND IT WAS SAFE TO
FEEL THE LOVE.

CHAPTER NINE:
THE OTHER SIDE OF COMPASSION

In the end, our efforts paid off and proved to set the stage for one of the richest, most spiritual experiences of my life. My heart did change in response to this experience with Kelly. I *was* able to *access my point of power* over and over again. My faith in my ability to cope with this loss resurrected my faith in being able to cope with life in general. I truly did experience the union with Kelly, and, other than one day of earthbound grief, I have felt great peace and love in my heart ever since.

I truly believe that, because I was equipped with the tools of tapping; was an expert in my understanding of the residual feelings from childhood which make themselves known through our children within and was able to access the wisdom of my higher guidance through the Akashic Records, I was able to not only "pre-grieve" while Kelly was still alive, but was also able to face the days after her death with much more ease.

I had already envisioned those moments; worked with them and neutralized them, so their actuality was not debilitating. The connection I felt with Kelly far outweighed any loss I felt on the physical plane. I was to find out soon that they same was true in my experience with Mom.

This is the last hug Kelly
and I experienced.
It was taken exactly 15 minutes
before the Vet arrived.

This picture alone quiets my doubts that this was not real. I was so grateful to my husband for capturing it. Today, as I look at it, I am in awe of how he captured our true bliss in knowing what was to occur. I look at the delight we both have-the absolute grace that is present, especially on my face! Whoever Kelly and I were at that precise moment-together we knew all of our efforts were going to pay off. And they did.

CHAPTER TEN:
THE TUNNEL AND BEYOND

Nothing prepared me for the experience I had the morning following Kelly's transition. This was the first email I sent to those who had shared their thoughts and prayers with us during this process.

Kelly successfully made her transition, and the following is what I have written so far. It obviously speaks for itself, but I wanted to take a moment to thank each and every one of you for your thoughts and prayers.

As could have been predicted, Kelly and I had a very powerful experience. The night of the actual passing was spent dealing with the emotions at hand. It was peaceful and beautiful, and we had a wonderful setting for her spirit to lift out of her body. I truly related to the event as more of a graduation than a "death."

This morning the meditations I have had with her are truly spectacular. When I awoke, I had a smile on my face and felt peace in my heart. I opened our Akashic Records and tuned into her energy. I was told that Kelly's essence had dispersed rather quickly. What I saw at that moment in my mind's eye was much like the sifting of flour. She just shook off her body like a dog and emerged as her soul essence.

I tuned into this etheric essence of Kelly. It was quite amazing. She showed me that she had left her body rather quickly then hovered above until it completely released. Just as we had practiced, our energy merged and began to expand together. As we were approaching the grid of unconditional love, which is where Kelly and I had gone in meditations over and over again in the last month as we prepared, I saw her go through the process of shaking off her body referenced above. I realized, later, that the grid was as far as I could take her in the prior meditations because that was all I knew.

Once there, Kelly was greeted by other beings and the essence of her next self which was a male figure.

(Note: I had gotten in earlier meditations that Kelly was positioning herself to step into human form. In fact, what the Records had shown me was that usually when a pet comes into a household which treats them as a human, they are preparing, in their evolutionary progression, to take on the density of human form soon. Until that time, I was told, most animals return to the group consciousness of the animal kingdom. But, as we have all been all things in the process of evolution of the soul, there comes a time when a pet has had enough incarnations to gather the density to become human. This was believable to me because when I lost my first pet, I saw this happen. But that was many moons ago, and back then, I did not understand and trust as I do now.)

As the meditation continued, the essence of Kelly turned to me, took the imprint of my heart, implanted it into hers and began her journey through the tunnel. Because I was an implant, I was able to go with her. Again, I saw it through Kelly's eyes. But it was like a near-death experience or something– Dannion Brinkley style!

When we started going through the tunnel, I began to cry and said, "Oh my god, I get to go through the tunnel with her!" It was exhilarating and wonderful. I did not feel afraid. I did not question it. It all made sense.

I got to see where she will reside and what she will be doing. And, because of the implant, we have access much like I have with my godchild who just moved to Paris. She's just a phone call away.

It was spectacular – breath-taking! I will never be the same.

Since then I have not felt disconnected. I think this is what Kelly and I had been working towards this whole last month. And I trust there will be many more wonderful connections with her in this new form.

This does not mean, however, I do not have the tears and the moments of ah when I wake up and do not have to feed her or take her out.

But they are manageable and do not last long.

I attribute this to my ability to process through the grief as it emerged which allowed me to be so present every step of the way. I plan to spend the next few weeks writing and recording this experience. It was one of the richest of my life.

So there you have it–our first report. My sister sent flowers–other friends tuned in and had their own experiences. I feel so much love that sometimes my heart feels too small.

For several days after this email, I was filled with mixed emotions. Sometimes I cried and felt sad. Other times I felt bliss. In hindsight, what I felt was not that different than the ebb and flow of feelings I had experienced in that month preceding Kelly's transition.

I did have one very difficult day, however. Kelly transitioned on Monday. When I woke up Wednesday morning I plummeted into the reality of everyday living, and I flat lined.

I felt so depressed, weepy and vulnerable. No matter how much I tried to tap the feelings away, they did not shift.

I called Darlene. In her infinite wisdom she explained that for the previous month I had been operating at such a heightened state of awareness that now that this event was over, Kelly had gotten to where she needed to go, and I had experienced the very thing I had worked so hard to experience, I was now crashing back into this reality, into this dimension of the earth plane.

She explained that the contrast of energy *is* flat. It *is* heavier when compared to the lighter vibration of the etheric realms in which I had been hanging out in over the past month. I had been in an expanded state of consciousness, but it was not one I could sustain.

I understood that. I didn't like it, but I understood it. It kept me in the moment instead of collapsing into an all-out state of despair.

On Thursday I once again awoke to a feeling of peace. I knew Kelly, and I had again been journeying together. We had had many conversations and connections. I had gone for my first run. I had reconnected to my body, and I once again felt secure on the earth plane.

I looked around my home and realized I no longer felt Kelly's presence. I felt her energy so present in the center of my heart. But nothing of hers in the physical realm now held her energy.

I would look at her bed and have no response. I glanced at her food bowl and felt no stir. The connection I had with her in my heart so far outweighed those objects that I truly did not experience a separation or loss.

I did, however, miss having a reason to get out of the house in the morning. But the feeling was generic – not specific to Kelly. I just did not feel sad that Kelly was not around for me to pet or take for walks. That void had been filled with the relationship and connection in the unseen we now had.

In fact, it was a bit unnerving.

Was I in denial? Could I really be this healthy? Had we really pulled this off? These thoughts flittered in the back of my mind, but they were more of a nuisance, like a mosquito flying around than thoughts which held any validity.

CHAPTER ELEVEN

A FINAL TRIBUTE TO MY DOG NAMED KELLY

We had taken our last walk.
Kelly had paused and pondered.
I had dropped her leash as I captured the moment.
It is at this exact place on earth that Kelly's ashes will be released.
I believe it is what she chose.

CHAPTER TWELVE:
READY TO RE-ENGAGE

Although I felt a little sheepish about doing this, I was compelled to go on the Internet to check out Rescue Shelters for dogs. I kept checking in with myself to see if I felt any pangs of guilt or disloyalty. But there were none.

I emailed several possibilities. There *was* one dog in particular which had grabbed my attention. His description was appealing. The picture looked a lot like Max. Both Max and Kelly were Border-Collie mixes. So is Averee.

I went back and looked at his information one more time. I saw a phone number, so I dialed it.

Elizabeth answered.

We talked about Averee and discussed making the necessary arrangements for me to come and meet him. She said she would call the next day.

I called Mom, Laurel, Cathy, Kim and Arthur and, with the excitement of a three-year-old, I screeched, *"I think I found us our next dog!"*

The next day came. She didn't call. It was this experience which proved to me this was not a desperate move to *"replace"* Kelly.

I did not panic. I did not feel tense. I stayed relaxed. I took a deep breath, did a few rounds of tapping and prayed that if Averee and I were meant to be together that the adoption would go through with ease. If not, I asked that it be blocked and prayed instead that I would be led to my next pet when the time was right.

Other than this I spent the day getting our home ready for a new pet. I dutifully laundered all of the bedding that was Kelly's. My daughter asked why. I replied, "It just feels respectful."

I was in awe that I could feel so receptive so quickly. But I also felt detached to the outcome of the present opportunity. I kept checking myself to make sure I was not trying to fill a void, ignoring vital feelings which needed to be faced with respect to Kelly and me.

Again, I felt this was the other side of compassion. Kelly and I had had the supreme luxury of walking through this promising challenge together. I knew other feelings might arise, but I had full confidence I could deal with them. I was sure Kelly and I would have many wonderful exchanges. I even believed it were possible that Kelly had a hand in leading me to Averee. I wasn't sure. I just felt if it did not work out with Averee he had served the purpose of showing me my heart was ready to re-engage.

It had taken me eighteen months to feel this way after losing Max.

The next day Laura called. She was the actual person who had been taking care of Averee. Within five minutes we knew it was a match and we made arrangements to meet.

We both had to drive about 2.5 hours. I seized the opportunity to revisit the entire experience Kelly, and I had shared. There were tears and moments of pride. My body inflated with warmth as I relived the last month we had shared, and my heart did not feel empty. It felt full.

When Laura and Averee arrived, I stepped out of my car to go meet him.

He jumped on the ground.

I bent down and received my first lick.

We put Averee in my trailblazer. The back seats were down and lined with doggie pillows and treats. He began his exploration while we took care of the necessary papers to complete the adoption.

Laura then tearfully told Averee goodbye, got back in her car and left. Averee jumped into the front seat and watched as she drove away. He then turned his head real quick, buried it into my chest and sought comfort. It felt completely natural to meet his need.

It wasn't five minutes into the drive home when he came up from behind and put his head over my shoulder as if he were giving me a hug.

Kelly had done that all of the time. I used to tell her that I didn't think I would ever find another dog who would hug me as she did. Part of me felt that Kelly was showing Averee the ropes. I imagined

Kelly greeting Averee and then instructing him on what I liked and how to win my favor.

If this were the case, she did a very thorough job. Averee could not be a better match.

The transition was complete.

Two weeks later the Vet called to say she had Kelly's ashes. When I actually saw them and touched them, I wept. I then noticed on the Cremation Certificate that the exact day of cremation had been November 19th. That was the Wednesday after her transition. It was the one day I had felt so much sadness and grief.

Averee and I took a walk around Lake Grace. Every few steps I would spread a few Kelly's remains. Kelly was now finally free.

CHAPTER FOURTEEN:
ON THE OTHER SIDE OF COMPASSION AWAITS YOUR BLISS

In less than one week I moved through the phases of grief and landed in the valley of acceptance and resolution. My heart had re-engaged. It truly was a graduation for both Kelly and me. Even that admission brings heartfelt tears of appreciation for the experience Kelly, and I were willing to share.

I attribute the swiftness of this to my willingness and ability to embrace what emerged within me and to neutralize the emotions with the energy tapping techniques of EFT.

CHAPTER FIFTEEN:
TAKING THE EXPERIENCE TO THE WORLD

As is my nature, when the dust settled, and I had acclimated to my life without Kelly, I began to write the story. Out of the story came the workshop.

My assistant and I sent in a proposal to a prestigious retreat center back east. The workshop was accepted and scheduled for the middle of August. Part of the marketing plan was to offer a series of Introductory Workshops around the country entitled, BEYOND COMPASSION: *"Accessing Your Point of Power During Loss."*

The first was scheduled for the middle of January in Syracuse, New York. My arrival date would be the 17th – exactly ninety days after Kelly had been set free.

CHAPTER SIXTEEN:
THE AMAZING
REALIZATION

I am driving down the freeway from Philadelphia to New York. The road is open. It is safe. I say my sacred prayer which aligns me with my higher guidance and immediately feel a presence. There is a council around me. In my mind's eye, I realize a meeting has convened.

I hear the voice of an Elder. *"It was not pre-determined, you understand. The experience you and your pet created evolved because of choice. You chose to move beyond your attachment. You chose to ask the questions regarding the higher purpose of what you were facing. And from those questions came the answers. You saw how Kelly's release could also be a release for you. You chose to examine your life with Kelly and to identify the lessons of your journey together.*

You could have chosen to become a victim to the grief and to wallow in the loss, thus missing the opportunity this situation offered. But instead, you used the tools you had acquired to cope with your fears. Your choice enabled you to assist both you and your pet in moving to your next respective levels of consciousness.

Understand it was your choice to deal with this situation in this manner. That choice allowed both of these elevations to occur.

The result was NOT pre-determined.

It evolved in response to the choices you made and the openness you sustained to the expansiveness of this experience.

You DID choose to access your point of power by neutralizing the pain and constantly moving into that ever-evolving state of empowerment, grace, and trust.

It is this that you are now to teach.

It is this that you will carry into all of the experiences in your life from now on."

The image in my mind's eye faded, and I was left to ponder what had just been revealed. It had been ninety days since Kelly's passing. Without putting any focus on my income or my work the month of December had been the best month of the whole year. I had quadrupled my income. To this day I believe it was a result of sustaining that higher vibration of love which then attracted the abundance into my life.

My heart had indeed been altered. My life out-pictured this truth as well.

SECTION TWO:
It's Show Time

CHAPTER SEVENTEEN:
THE DELIVERY

Not long after I returned from my trip back east, I received an email from Gregg Braden's website announcing he would be offering a workshop at the Agape Spiritual Center in the Los Angeles area. Michelle and Ryan lived in L.A. I had wanted to visit them ever since I had married them. I had also wanted to present Gregg with a copy of this story. I knew I would not have been able to achieve what I had without the guidance of his words which was what inspired me to dedicate this work to him.

I decided to hand-deliver the booklet. I registered for the workshop and booked my flight to head west. I was to leave on Thursday, February 26th.

On Sunday, February 22nd, I was awakened by a call.

"Cathy, this is Gene. Listen, your Mom just fell. She is at the County hospital, but they are getting ready to transport her to Grand Island where they will operate."

Gene is Mom's yard man, friend, and confidant. He was the first name on her responder list for her life line. Mom had fallen out of bed early that morning. Close enough to the phone she had dialed 911. Within minutes they responded. She had indeed broken her right hip.

Four years earlier she had broken her left hip. She had recuperated from that fall. With a pacemaker, four months of physical therapy and my driving from Minnesota to Nebraska each weekend to assist she had recovered and had moved back home.

My siblings and I all knew she was only as good as her next fall. When I heard the words Gene spoke, I immediately felt it was the beginning of the end.

I also knew I was not in a position to travel that distance every week as I had been four years earlier. My situation was different now. I had a position at a job I really liked which would prohibit me from making the weekly trips down to help Mom rehabilitate. Indeed, it did feel like the beginning of the end.

I *was* able to clear my schedule for a few days. Within 45 minutes, I had thrown some clothes and Averee in the car, and we were on our way to Nebraska. Once in the quiet of my car, the shock set in. I cried most of the way down.

It was unknown as to whether Mom would survive the operation. As I drove to Nebraska, she was on her way to the hospital where the procedure could take place. They had been notified to wait until a family member could arrive. My older brother, who lives an hour away from Mom, was in Kansas and could not be reached. My younger brother, who lives two hours away, was in Georgia and could not be reached. I had been reached and was on my way. It was an eight-hour drive.

I did a lot of energy tapping as I drove from point A to point B. I tried to neutralize the shock, the grief, the fear. I did meditations in which I brought Mom's spirit into my mind's eye. I gave her permission to go if that is what she desired. I said my good-byes in the unseen which allowed me to do some of the pre-grieving sequences so I would be prepared for the worst.

I *was* able to reach my sister in California. I assured her I would keep her posted. And finally, I reached my niece. She lived in Denver, six hours away. After her tears had subsided she stated simply, "I am coming. I will throw the kids in the car and leave right away." I did not realize until that moment how alone I had really felt. Her words were like milk and cookies for my soul.

As I neared the exit that would take me to the hospital where Mom laid my thoughts raced. I wondered if she would survive the operation. I wondered how she would respond. And I wondered if I would have to cancel my trip to L.A.

43

CHAPTER EIGHTEEN:
THE, "OH MY GOD" MOMENT!

As I took my exit, I decided to give the hospital a quick call. I wanted to find out what room Mom was in and get an idea of what to expect. I was connected to the floor nurse. She reported that Mom was fine. "She's in recovery. The operation went fine."

My mouth dropped. "Operation," I gasped. "I thought they were going to wait until a family member could get there."

"Your Mother opted to get it done. She signed the papers herself."

I didn't know whether to be relieved or angry. My first thought was what if Mom would have died on the table and there would have been no family member present!

And yet, I must admit I was relieved. I had dreaded standing in the waiting room alone waiting for the results.

I resolved the complexity of feelings and, with a smile on my face, felt resigned to the fact that, even in this state, Mom was still in charge.

When I walked into her room, she was surprisingly alert and responsive. When she saw me, she shook her head and winced, "I really messed up this time."

I returned the smile and replied, "We'll get through it."

I stayed with her until the medicine kicked in and she fell asleep. My niece, Cathy finally arrived, and we all drove the twenty minutes to where Mom lived.

I spent the next few days driving between Mom's home and the hospital twenty miles away. Mom's spirits were good as long as someone was with her. She was obviously scared, however, and upset that this had occurred.

If I had any hope of making my trip to L.A. I had to leave by Tuesday.

I was torn. Part of me wanted to drop everything and just stay with Mom. However, I knew my job would not survive that choice- and I wanted to follow through with my trip.

The tension of that decision was eased in a conversation with my brother, John. He said something that set the stage for the months to come.

"Cathy, you have to let Mom struggle with this herself so she can make the decision whether to stay or go. She can't do that if she doesn't have time alone. You can't rescue her from this choice, none of us can."

God, I knew what he said was true. But I have never had such a difficult time letting go and letting it be. The worst moment was on Tuesday night when we were all getting ready to go.

I knew I had to make it to John's place in Omaha by 8:00 PM that night if I had any hope of making it back for work the next day. That meant I had to be on the road by about 6:00 PM. My sister-in-law and her daughter were there as well. When we all got ready to leave Mom looked at me and said, "You're not going are you?"

My heart sank. I explained that in order to get back to work the next day I had to drive to John's that night. She begged me to stay just for a while after everyone else had gone. It was not common for my mother to beg anyone for anything.

Once we were alone, she told me how scared she was and how she did not want to stay there alone. She was somewhat delusional. "If you leave I don't know who will take care of me."

I explained the nurses would be there to tend to her needs. "But I don't know them." She replied.

I told her I would stay for awhile. But anytime I would get ready to go she would again beg me to stay.

Thinking the medication would take hold soon I promised her I would wait until she fell asleep. Her eyes got as big as saucers as she dug in her heels apparently determined not to fall asleep.

9:00 PM came. She was still wide awake. I knew I had to get on the road. I broke into tears as I explained I just had to go, "Mom, I just can't afford to miss work."

I have never seen my mother so frightened.

I called in the nurses attempting to make her feel safe. I kissed her goodbye and reluctantly got on the road.

I knew Mom had to confront this struggle herself. She had to have an idea of what her life would be like if she opted to stay. It was a battle between her and her soul, and I had no business interfering.

But the fear in her eyes followed me all the way home.

CHAPTER NINETEEN:
THE COMPLEXITY OF LIFE

As I boarded the plane that would take me to L.A., I heard this haunting voice nagging on my consciousness, *"How can you go to L.A.? Mom is fighting for her life. You should be there – you should be there by her side. She is deciding whether to stay or go."*

It was surreal.

As I landed at LAX and felt the California air on my face, the voice became mute. It was like getting a soul massage. I felt comforted by the elements. I was full of anticipation for the upcoming workshop and for the opportunity to present Gregg with my story about Kelly. It had not yet occurred to me that our story was the precursor to the story which was unfolding for me regarding Mom.

The time with Ryan and Michelle was the frosting on the proverbial cake.

When I walked into the Agape Spiritual Center and went into the sanctuary, I was vehemently surprised. The workshop was small and intimate. Gregg was now talking to crowds which numbered in the thousands. This crowd was more like several hundred at most. I marveled at how perfect it was that he would be so approachable. I sat three rows back. At the first break, I seized the opportunity to approach him. No one else was around.

I expressed how much I valued his work and stated I had actually met him over twelve years ago in San Rafael. He replied that he remembered my face. "I am bad on names, but I never forget a face."

The distance between us diminished. I handed him the booklet. I explained how it was dedicated to him because his work and video, "Walking Between The Worlds" had been so instrumental in the success of my journey with Kelly.

We had a very sweet exchange. I felt tremendous gratitude to the Universe for providing the opportunity for such intimacy. I left L.A. feeling ready to take to the world the message learned from the transformation Kelly and I had experienced.

CHAPTER TWENTY:
ACCORDING TO GOD'S WILL

However, to no surprise, a different plan was about to unfold. I did not take my message to the world. Instead, over the next several months, I used every hour of sick time I had traveling back and forth between Nebraska and Minnesota tending to Mom's needs.

It did not pay to be away from her. The tension I felt prohibited me from accomplishing much anyway. The days I did have to return to my life in Minnesota gave Mom the time she needed to struggle with her choice. We both, however, felt the most calm when I was sitting in the chair next to her hospital bed.

She did have bouts of healing which enabled her to leave the hospital and go to a rehabilitation center. But once there the demands of that program would wear her down. She would end up back in the hospital with a new ailment or strain. Her lungs were weak. Her heart was weak. Her body was simply unable to sustain a level of strength.

She did gain enough stamina, however, to be transported back to the hospital in her hometown. She prospered there. She had her support system there. Her Doctor of twenty years could tend to her needs. Her friends could visit. Her surroundings were familiar. It is a small town. The nurses called her by her first name and Mom once again felt safe.

Still, it was touch and go. We had many close calls when it seemed the time had come for Mom to crossover to the other side. But she kept pulling through. Her Doctor once remarked that she didn't have nine lives. She had more like twenty-five.

Easter Sunday came and went and her birthday approached. She would be 93. My sister flew in from California, and all four of us met at the hospital to help Mom celebrate.

We took a family photo which ended up being our last.

The following Sunday was Mother's Day. My older brother owned a restaurant, and he always held a Mother's Day buffet. My sister and I wanted to take Mom to the buffet one last time. She rallied enough to go and appeared quite regal in her attire.

One of their featured items on their menu is Mom's recipe for carrot cake. It does literally melt in your mouth. When my sister was standing in line, she overheard a woman in front of her remark that she wanted to save enough room for that carrot cake.

Suzy tapped her on the shoulder. "That's my mother's recipe." She proudly stated. "In fact, Mom, who just celebrated her 93rd birthday, is here enjoying the buffet as well."

Once the woman had finished her meal, she came over to our table and introduced herself. She complimented Mom on her recipe. Mom beamed with pride. She was once again in her element. The gifts she offered to the world were being recognized. That acknowledgment was the best Mother's Day present Mom could have received.

CHAPTER TWENTY-ONE:
MAYBE THERE IS HOPE

Mom appeared to be gaining strength, and it looked as though we could attempt to move her to an assisted-living facility. On June 1st, my brother, Tom, and I packed her things and got Mom settled in her new home. It appeared as though she had stabilized. Our hope was that she would be able to settle in for awhile.

Unfortunately, it lasted only ten days. The day after my sixty-first birthday I got the call that she had again been taken to the hospital. She had developed pneumonia. The prognosis did not look good.

When I managed to speak to her on the phone, she asked how soon I could come. I cleared my schedule. Within a few days, I was once again by her side.

She did stabilize again. I swear she was like the energizer bunny. Just when we would think it was the beginning of the end she would twist and turn and re-enlist.

And then on June 22nd, two events collided and changed the charter course that would ultimately take her home.

CHAPTER TWENTY-TWO:
ONE DOOR CLOSES –
ANOTHER DOOR OPENS!

I was fortunate in that my private work was not location-dependent. The majority of my consultations were done by phone. My part-time job, however, was not. It was my dream job. The site was located right across the street from where I lived. It was a thirty-two-hour position but required my only being on-site approximately ten hours a week. I ran an Outpatient clinic for early recovering addicts. It had been opened in late 2006. The hope was that the Clinic would grow and would necessitate hiring more staff.

Because of a series of events unrelated to this story it never happened. We had struggled to stay open. The low population had actually made it more feasible for me to take the 157 hours of sick time I ended up using in response to the crisis with Mom. But there was always this impending doom that Headquarters would decide to close its doors.

On the morning of June 22nd, the email came from my Supervisor warning me that this would most likely be the case. The lease for our office was up in October, and the likelihood that the program would close was eminent.

The dreaded news had arrived.

Two hours later I received a call from Mom's Doctor. He said that Mom had stabilized enough to leave acute care but did not have the strength to return to assisted-living. We, as a family, needed to decide what came next. She either needed to stay in the hospital for private pay or would have to be transferred to a nursing home. The decision had to be made within a week.

The synchronicity of these two events was unreal.

I felt pulled. I put on my running shoes and hit the trails which never failed to offer clarity.

Even though Headquarters was not planning to close the clinic for three more months, I knew that I only had four clients. Two of them were about to graduate. One was on the brink of relapse and being discharged, and the fourth had just been readmitted and could be transferred to another program with ease. This reality weighed against the fact that Mom could return to her home if she had twenty-four-hour care.

With each step that my feet hit the ground, I became more firmly planted in my decision. It was time for me to take care of my Mom. It was time to bring her home.

I called my boss and explained the situation. "It doesn't make sense for me to wait until October when Mom and my family need me now. I know it means closing early, but the writing appears to be on the wall."

He agreed.

I put a call into Roger, Mom's Doctor. I ran it by him. He also agreed, wholeheartedly. "I could not feel better about this option. It offers the best circumstances for your Mom to heal."

The respective arrangements were made.

I gathered everything I would need for the next three months to relocate to Nebraska. On the drive down I once again spoke with Mom's Doctor. I mentioned that I did not know how long I could commit to this, but I knew I was able to at least pull it off for three months. I asked him how she was doing that day and he laughed and said, "You know, today she looked great." I laughed as well and said,

"Mom has wanted me to move in with her for the past five years. Knowing her, I will get down there, and she will last another six years!" We laughed. Then he replied, "I will be surprised if she is not sick again by September."

I was not sure what I was getting myself into, but I knew it was the right choice. I marveled at how the Universe had shut one door I had fought to keep from closing and opened another that I had been struggling with to keep ajar.

CHAPTER TWENTY-THREE:
THE DALAI MAMA!

There was a certain magic that took place when I got Mom settled back in her home. About a week later I wrote the following piece for my newsletter. It captures our life together.

"I recently made the decision to temporarily move from my home in the Twin Cities to the middle of Nebraska thinking I was coming to help my 93-year-old mother prepare for and make her transition to another side.

Instead, it appears as though she has re-enlisted.

She is amazing–this mother of mine. She is in a total state of bliss.

When she was first released from the hospital, her Doctor had recommended hospice. But at her first follow-up appointment, he assessed, with pleasure, that hospice was not appropriate at this time. She is now simply in home health care which means, besides intermittent health care support, it is just Mom and me.

I grind all of her favorite foods, so she does not aspirate, and I respond to her every need without hesitation or delay.

Other than this, I watch. I study. I learn.

My cousin was over last night. Mom told him she could not be happier to be home. Then, she glanced over at me and added, "I am not sure Cathy is happy about it–but I sure am."

I laughed and said, "No, I would not be here if I did not want to be. I am too damn old to do anything I do not want to do." He and I laughed. Mom smiled. Then I added, "It is a gift being with her at this point in her life. I lovingly call her the Dalai Mama! She is ZEN personified."

And this is true. It is simply amazing to watch her–yes, even study her. She is at home, literally and figuratively, and she is modeling for me how to be the same.

She is, at this time in my life, my greatest teacher. She is teaching me how to just be–at the moment–totally fulfilled for what each moment offers, without expectation, without disappointment.

Heart-filled seconds–thankful to just be–feet are bobbing, in child-like fashion, she closes her eyes and sleeps in her recliner.

Unadulterated joy exudes from the heart of her soul right out the bottoms of her feet!

I asked her once if she were afraid to die. She paused and said, "No, not really–I just love living so much I don't want to leave."

It feels so gratifying to be here with her that I called my best friend the other day and asked if she thought perhaps I was hiding from my own life because this felt so good. Having been through this with her own father, she assured me that was not the case. "It is just so relaxing to be in their presence… there are peace and serenity that seldom we get to see."

I know at some point the end will come–maybe next week–maybe in a month or so–maybe not even for a year–but each moment is a gif– it is a dance we do as we waltz through her daily routine of meds and exercises and short trips to the bathroom with oxygen in hand.

A high school friend, who lives down the street, links me to the outside world. A baby monitor provides Mom and me the freedom to be away from each other while still in touch. My work-out equipment, computers, printers and all of my office paraphernalia have taken over her basement. I continue to write, to do my radio show, phone consults, and even on-line webinars.

But I am always listening.

I have become familiar with her sounds; the crackling noise of her opening her favorite piece of candy; a cough which summons me to offer her a sip of water; the sound of her sighing as she watches the birds outside, but mostly the sound of her breathing.

The other day I had the monitor close by when I was doing my daily sit-ups. All of a sudden I realized I was pacing myself to her rhythmic breaths. It was like being back in the womb–magnificent–breath-giving–spellbinding.

Yes, I am forever listening–as if I am her higher Guardian–just a whisper away. She calls my name, and I am within seven seconds of responding.

At this time in each of our lives, we are dance partners, and our dance cards are full. It is just her and me–me and my dog and me and my work. What a reprieve from my day-to-day world. In this small town in the middle of Nebraska where there are two stop lights, one grocery store, and health food is Kraft cheddar cheese and Jiffy peanut butter–I am learning how just to be.

And so it was. Home Health Care provided support. They bathed her and medically monitored her. The rest was up to me.

CHAPTER TWENTY-FOUR:
OUR LIFE TOGETHER

I came to cherish the life Mom and I created. I often drew from the experience with Kelly and recognized that Mom and I were establishing the same force field of love. However, unlike the situation with Kelly, in which a specific date was established for her transition, with Mom, the outcome was unknown.

At times this was unnerving.

How long could I commit to this lifestyle? I had agreed to stay with Mom at least until October. But I knew in my heart of hearts I would now never be able to turn away from her and send her to a nursing home.

When I spoke with Roger or even my siblings, we would agree that, if and when the time came that I had to go, we would figure something out.

But inside I knew if I had to leave Mom now it would be the most difficult decision of my life and the biggest lesson I could ever encounter.

Often I prayed this would not to be the case. "Please do not make me have to confront that situation. I just could not bear to turn away from her now."

But then I would have moments when I feared it would not feel magical, but instead, would feel burdensome. I dreaded the possibility that the day might come when the love I felt in my heart would turn to regret and resentment.

I wavered between these two extremes, but as the days went by, I adjusted my thoughts to the probability that this would most likely go on beyond October. I assured my family, as well as myself that I was in for the long haul.

Arthur had taken a two-bedroom flat that was closer to his work and the kid's school. We had spoken of renting out our shared condo for six months. I was definitely preparing myself to make Nebraska my home for awhile.

Mom and I even talked about making one last trip to Lake Tahoe. She was doing so well. The subject at least warranted the conversations.

As August drew closer, however, it did become clear to me that what I would not be able to do the workshop I had contracted to lead back east.

I had not been able to do the marketing that was planned. The thought of organizing the five-day workshop seemed overwhelming. With regret in my heart, I called the facility and expressed my concerns.

It was time to make a decision, and the only one that felt right was to cancel. When I emailed my contact person, I said, "Offering a workshop entitled, *Accessing Your Point Of Power During Loss,*" at this time seems a bit premature. Intuitively I feel the last chapter of this program has yet to be written."

She was familiar with the situation with Mom. She agreed and assured me I could resubmit a proposal when the time felt right.

My sister's plane ticket to come and cover that week, however, had already been purchased, and she was committed to coming out nonetheless.

Suddenly the week I had planned on flying back east was now open for me to do something else–to get a break from my responsibilities and to give my sister and Mom some time on their own.

Every possibility seemed to get blocked except the one of my returning to Minnesota and taking a vacation in my own home.

I was amazed at how comforting this option turned out to be. It reminded of how much I loved living in our little condo. I had experienced sufficient distance from the job across the street so that returning home did not trigger any residual grief. It was comforting to realize that transition had been made. My vacation at home also gave Arthur and me a chance to reconnect. I met with friends and went on hikes and re-acquainted myself with the life I had left behind.

When the time came to return to Nebraska, I felt renewed. I was ready to put an ad in the paper and to sub-lease the condo for six months.

I returned that Friday. My cousin was visiting. While I was gone, Mom had actually been re-admitted to the hospital. She had become dehydrated from the diuretics she had been taking to clear the fluid from her lungs. It was not serious. My sister had handled it, and Mom seemed to be in good spirits when I returned.

CHAPTER TWENTY-FIVE:
THE UNEXPECTED FALL FROM GRACE

I returned to Mom's home the night before my sister was to fly back to California. I wanted one last good night of uninterrupted sleep, so I went to bed early. Mom, Suzy, and Mark were still up watching something on TV, but I was exhausted. I kissed Mom good night–bid Suzy and Mark good night and went downstairs to sleep on the couch.

I awoke about 4 A.M. I couldn't sleep. I moved upstairs and slept on the couch in the family room. I had just dozed off when I heard a sound. It was Suzy. She had gone to the bathroom, but when she returned and saw I was awake, she whispered, "Mom fell last night. We are back in her bedroom. We don't think anything is broken."

My heart sank. My mind was full of questions. How bad was it? Why didn't you wake me up? I ran back to Mom's bedroom. When she saw me, she gave me a faint smile and just shook her head in disbelief.

Suzy said Mom had refused to go to the hospital. "I would have awakened you, but you seemed to be in such a deep sleep. I knew I was leaving tomorrow and you would have to carry the brunt of the responsibility. I wanted you to get one last night of good sleep."

She further explained that she had called downstairs for my cousin to come and help her move Mom from the bathroom where she fell to her bedroom. I could not believe I had not heard her then. Something deep within me knew I had been "kept" asleep. For whatever reason, what had transpired between Mom and Suzy was an exchange only they were to experience.

Mom was put on morphine for the pain. The first set of x-rays confirmed nothing was broken. The time came for Suzy and Mark to leave. They had to catch their planes home. Suzy considered just staying, but the outcome was unknown, and she had commitments she had to tend to back in California.

I was in shock. I was heart-broken this had taken such an abrupt turn.

CHAPTER TWENTY-SIX:
HOW DID THIS HAPPEN?

Roger, Mom's faithful Doctor, dropped in after Church. We had just seen him that previous week. We had mentioned wanting to take our trip to Lake Tahoe. The look on his face now said it all. "How did this happen?" He appeared as disappointed as I.

There were no answers. However, his question gave form to the one that was raging in my own head.

As I sat there in the hospital watching Mom breathe in and out, I grabbed my computer and tried to capture what I felt. The following is what came out.

So here I sit – not in the comfort of the home Mom and I were to share for the next several months – but in a hospital room where I sit alone staring at a body whose spirit is riding the bus to the unseen.

Damn, I thought we had more time. I had acclimated myself to the idea that Mom was doing so grand that I adjusted my plans so I could stay with her into the New Year.

I returned from my last trip to Minnesota where I had gathered the last of my important items so I could transition with ease. I was prepared to build my internet empire as Mom prepared to go to the other side. I thought that was the deal we had made.

How did this happen?

How did we move into this phase so abruptly?

I was intellectually ready for it – but I truly thought we were in for the long haul.

Instead, it appears to be brief – 7 to 10 days I am told.

She had had a few bouts of her lungs filling up, but we had resolved that. In fact, she had just returned from a two-day stay in the hospital the day after I returned from Minnesota.

When she came home she did say she felt a little wobbly, but her spirits were good, and she was happy, alert and communicative.

Then, while in the bathroom, she lost her balance, her feet went out, and she went down. It was so fast, so unexpected.

I am struggling to understand. I trust this is meant to be, but there are many selves within me that do not agree. They are not adjusting graciously to this fate. They are fearful, angry and feel cheated by this situation.

Too much of me is not yet ready to let her go. I know I have all of the tools at my disposal to deal with this. But I am, at this moment, too angry at the situation to apply them.

Later that day Mom's pain was not subsiding. They decided to take another set of X-rays. This time they x-rayed her pelvis. It had indeed been fractured. There was bleeding going on internally. It was this injury which was causing Mom so much pain.

By the next time, Roger came in the prognosis had worsened. "She has gone into renal failure. At most," he said, "She has a few days."

Within twenty-four short hours, my whole life had taken a turn. Yes, I knew it could happen—but it just came so unexpectedly. I had a hard time letting go.

CHAPTER TWENTY-SEVEN: I CAN'T SHAKE THIS ANGER!

I wasn't angry that Mom fell. We all knew Mom was just as good as her next incident. I was angry at the situation. And, as accomplished as I am at dealing with feelings, I was the least prepared of all.

I called my friend Kim. I was in tears. "I need help. I can't shake this feeling."

Just as we had done in the situation with Kelly Kim once again helped me deal with this grief. She began to state the sequences. I tearfully repeated her words and tapped on the respective end points. The knot in my stomach began to loosen. The stress seemed more removed, but it was still there. It was time to return to the hospital. I felt more clear. But there was still a sense of uneasiness and a fear of the unknown.

When I got back to the hospital, Mom appeared tranquil. I called my friend Laurel. As we talked, I stated I was still not shaking this. "Just hang in there, Cathryn. You will. You always do. You find some positive twist that takes you to a new place, and then you recommit."

I am not sure what other words were exchanged. I just know there was that moment when my perception shifted. We were still on the phone. "You know what Laurel it just shifted. I am looking at Mom, and I realize we are now in the *Kelly phase*. I have to relate to her telepathically now. The time for conversations has passed. She is spending more time in the other world. I have to now connect to her in that dimension so, when she does let go, I can see her to the other side. God, Laurel, my energy just shifted. I know how to do this part."

I could not tell you exactly what had taken place in those conversations. All I know is that the combination of those two calls with my friends allowed a shift. The part of me who had spent the last ten years of my life and Mom's preparing for this moment stepped on center stage, and from then on, that part of me was in charge.

CHAPTER TWENTY-EIGHT:
THE LAST HOURS

It was about 11:00 AM. Mom was restless. She kept struggling. At times she would gesture for me to come and scratch her back. I would dutifully position my hand beneath her shoulders and begin to rub back and forth gently.

On this particular occasion, Mom looked up at me. She smiled. I then noticed tears were gently falling on her cheeks. They were not tears of fear or regret but rather tears of release–tender and soft–as if her weeping was a sign of relief.

I pulled her gently to me and held her. The bed railing was between us, but I maneuvered myself, so I could comfortably support her. Tears began to fall down my cheeks as well.

I spoke softly – almost in a whisper. I told her it was okay to go. I assured her we would carry on and we would be alright. I told her how much we loved her and reminded her that she would live on in all of us, "Every time we wipe out a sink or make mashed potatoes or prepare a care package for someone we love, it will be in memory of you."

I reminded her to watch for the Light and to follow those whom she would recognize. And I told her how very much I loved her and how wonderful the last several months had been.

Her tears fell gently on my shoulder and then she closed her eyes. The words ceased. They were no longer necessary. I just held her.

Several nurse aides walked in, but I motioned for them to please leave us be.

The exception was Carol, the hospice nurse. In the last two months, she had become a friend and a confidant. Seeing her face was indeed a welcomed relief.

I remarked that if Mom and I were home, I would climb into bed with her and just hold her. She replied, "Well you can do that here."

And so I did. Carol helped me position myself so as not to cramp Mom. I climbed in beside her and just held her as she peacefully slept.

Those moments were precious – and her scent – how I loved her scent.

I would have assumed the smell of death would have been pungent. But Mom's scent was the smell of bread rising. It must have been the yeast in her body, but its sweetness brought back the memories of her baking her infamous holiday lambs. It made her kindness tangible and filled the stark, hospital room with love.

Our breathing became synchronized and, for that brief time, we were one. I can still close my eyes and return to that experience. I take a deep breath, and it is as if I inhale pure, unadulterated love. That photo memory is forever etched in my brain.

The author in me began to write the story in my head. What a wonderful ending, I mused. It felt as though Mom were going to slip over to the other side right then and there.

"Yes, this is indeed fitting."

As time went by I decided to watch a movie while she rested in my arms. Mom and I loved to watch movies together. "How romantic that we could watch one last movie at this time," I thought. I reached for the TV control that is always attached to a hospital bed. I turned the TV on and found the Lifetime Channel. I could not tell you what was playing, but I watched until, I, too, fell asleep.

No one bothered us. Carol had put a sign on the door that read, "No visitors." Mom and I were between the two worlds–together–in our own little cocoon.

I cherished each minute–for the first several hours–then the experience took a turn.

CHAPTER TWENTY-NINE:
FROM THE MAGICAL TO THE COMICAL TO THE RELEASE

My body began to cramp. I had to go the bathroom. The dialogue in my head took a turn.

Instead of cherishing each moment I began thinking, "Okay, Mom this would be a great time to go. You know how to do this. Just lift up. Just lift up and find your loved one's hand. It is time to go to the Light now."

But nothing happened. Mom's breaths were soft and gentle, but they were still there.

I tried to "zen" my way through the cramping but to no avail.

Soon, it became comical. I felt as though I were caught in a Seinfeld episode, a scenario George might find himself in – or Elaine.

Finally, I surrendered to the reality that Mom was going to go on her own time. My Kodak moment had come to an end.

I maneuvered myself over the railing.

Mom turned to me with a look of wonder in her eyes. I hugged her and whispered softly that I was just going to the bathroom.

She nodded then once again closed her eyes.

By the time I returned she had fallen back into that place of serene bliss. The look on her face was divine.

She remained that way for the next eight hours. No one came into the room. I left for brief moments, but mostly, I watched, and I waited.

Around 9:00 PM she began to fidget and moan. Her breathing became erratic. I called for the nurse. They gave her medicine to regulate her breathing and increased the morphine to manage her pain.

She pulled at her clothes as though she were trying to remove them. I had heard that when a person gets close to crossing over, they often tug at their clothes. It is supposedly a gesture which signals they are trying to get out of their body. The nurse thought she was hot and turned on a fan.

It took several hours, but Mom finally settled down and, once again, returned to that blissful state.

I was exhausted. I got ready to sleep in the bed beside her. I kissed her forehead, said goodnight, and, for what turned out to be the last time, told her I loved her.

The minute my head hit the pillow I fell into this deep sleep. It was 12:15.

Five minutes later I awoke to see the nurse standing next to Mom's body with her stethoscope. I asked if Mom were gone. She nodded, "Yes."

In just five minutes Mom had slipped away into the abyss.

The nurse left. I called Suzy and asked that she call Tom and John. I called my friend Carol. She was five minutes away. Without missing a beat, she said, "I'll be right up."

While I waited, I went and stood by Mom's body. It was already cold. It was obvious she was not there. But there was this warmth in the room. There was this energy in the air.

I called Darlene. It was only 10:30 PM in California where she lives. I told her Mom had passed and asked if she could verify how it went.

There was a moment of silence and then she said, "I have witnessed many transitions, but I have never seen anyone crossover with such joy. There is a whole coliseum of loved ones greeting her. She is overwhelmed with love and joy."

I left that hospital feeling as though I had just participated in a delivery. My heart was full – my spirit high.

CHAPTER THIRTY:
THE AFTERMATH

I was puzzled, though, how, after such an intimate exchange, I could have slept through Mom's actual release? I didn't have much time to ponder this, however. Carol arrived at the hospital. We gathered Mom's belongings and said our last good-byes.

One item I cherished was the pillow upon which Mom's head had laid. It was the pillow she had slept on at home. The night she was taken by ambulance to the hospital the medics had evidently grabbed this pillow to stabilize her head. It still had the same pillow slip on it. It held the essence of Mom. It held the memories of all the nights I helped put her to bed during the two months I was her caregiver. It now became my transitional object – a piece of Mom, a source of comfort which I could take home.

Carol went back to Mom's house with me. That was the one experience I did not want to face alone.

We talked about the last several months. Carol had been one of the few who had witnessed the magic between Mom and me. When I referenced the force field of love I felt that had been created between Mom and me, Carol understood.

After a stiff cup of coffee and shared memories and laughs, Carol left, and I prepared to sleep in Mom's house for the first night without her. I grabbed Mom's pillow and held it close to my belly. I slept with it for the next month. It gave the part of me who was not yet ready to let go something on which to hold.

CHAPTER THIRTY-ONE: THE CELEBRATION OF MOM'S LIFE

The next few days were filled with warm memories mixed with smiles and tears. I would pick something of Mom's up and would feel the tender pull of missing her. I would hear her voice every time I failed to turn the light on the stove off when done— or forgot to wipe out the sink. Mom's imprint was still very active in my head.

But there were also tasks to complete. The first task was to clear everything out of the house that reminded me of Mom's infirmity.

The first to go was the oxygen – then the walkers. I threw both of them in the trunk of her car until I could get rid of them. I did the same with the bed railing. All of the items which had made her last days comfortable very quickly became an irritant to me. I wanted the house to be only filled with signs of her well-lived life.

I then conferred with everyone about the funeral arrangements and began to make the calls which needed to be made. All of the details were addressed. By Friday, Suzy, Tom and John had arrived. We went to the funeral home, picked out the casket and made the final plans.

The family started arriving. I opted to stay down at the local Motel. I needed time to ponder the actual "Celebration of Life" message I was to deliver at the funeral. Ten years earlier Mom had asked if I would officiate her funeral. We had written the obituary which I dutifully delivered to the respective newspapers. Our pre-planning made every go quite smoothly. It was comforting to know that Mom's last wishes were being honored.

We were all clear we wanted the funeral to be a celebration of joy. It was an amazing dance the four of us did together. Each of us had our strong suit and Mom's "Celebration of Life" came off exactly as planned. It was full of humorous anecdotes, lovely music, and tear-filled remembrances.

Family and friends alike shared delightful stories. Many commented how it was the best funeral they had every attended. Joy permeated the room.

CHAPTER THIRTY-TWO:
NOW WHAT?

The day following the funeral all of the family had to go. I had agreed to stay and write the thank you notes and take care of the residue of tasks.

I found, however, I was dragging my feet. Facing all of those thank you notes seemed more than I could bear. On Wednesday night I turned in early and watched movies in bed. I must have fallen asleep quite soon. The next thing I knew I woke up and the clock read 5:30 AM.

I was elated. Seldom do I sleep that late or for that many hours. I jumped out of bed and felt refreshed for the first time in months.

I made a fresh pot of coffee and readied myself for the day. At one point I went to warm something up in the microwave and noticed the clock. It said 9:30.

Puzzled, I looked at the clock on my computer. Sure enough, it said 9:30. I looked outside. It was dark. Was it only 9:30 PM? Had I only slept an hour or two? I couldn't believe it!

I called my sister. "What time is it out there?" She laughed and said, "Two hours earlier than there!" "Okay, smart ass, I replied, "Just what time is it." She confirmed it was 7:30 PM Pacific Standard Time. I was in Central Standard Time.

I had only slept for two hours! I told Suzy what I had done. We laughed and hung up.

Since I had thought it was the morning I had already had my first cup of coffee. I was too wired to go back to bed. I grabbed the thank you notes; cranked the air conditioning up; turned the fireplace on and said to myself, "Okay, Mom. If anything will bring you back from the grave this will! Let's do these things together."

I wrote for three hours. Finally at 1:30 AM, with the last one written, I went back to bed.

By Friday all had been done. I packed my bags; took the copies of the tapes of the funeral and Averee and I hit the road. We took the trip to Lake Tahoe that Mom and I had spent so many hours planning. Every mile held a memory, and each memory was punctuated with a tear, a chuckle or a smile.

CHAPTER THIRTY-THREE:
WHERE'S THE GRIEF?

By the time I crossed the California state line. However, it had appeared as though many of the feelings had run their course. I noticed something felt very odd. As I wrote in my journal the next morning, it became clear.

Today while driving along the shores of Lake Tahoe I began to wonder why I was not having more of a reaction to being here without Mom.

The last time I was here was with Mom. Many of my adult memories here include Mom. In the last several months we had spent hours talking about taking one more road trip to Tahoe — so why, now that I am here, am I not having more melancholy feelings about her passing.

Tears began to fall upon my cheeks gently. I realized that Mom and I were not yet separated. In the last several months Mom and I had created a force field, and the vibration which sustained that force field was pure love. It was that love that carried her home, and it is that love which now keeps us connected.

It is the same kind of love a mother feels for her child for the first year of that newborn's life. I remember reading once that the reason this connection that exists this first year between mother and child is so strong is that the force field which is created while the child is in the womb continues in the etheric field after the child is born. That is why a mother, even if she is miles away, knows if her baby is crying.

Mom and I had created that kind of connection. One time a friend had dropped by, and we left the house for a few minutes to do an errand. When we had accomplished the task, he said he wanted to run out to his farm for a few minutes just to show it to me. I asked him how long it would take. He replied, "About fifteen minutes." We started heading down the country road that would take us there and all of a sudden I said, "I don't feel good about this. I think I need to get home."

Sure enough when I returned Mom had gotten up to go to the bathroom and, still too weak to lift her body up, was sitting on the commode unable to get off. Intuitively I had known she was in trouble. My gut sensed it. We were that connected in the unseen.

Even though she has now crossed over, we are still connected. She is in that higher vibration, but we are still linked energetically. We are still adjusting to the new arrangement. We ARE taking one last road trip to Tahoe. She is vibrationally connected to me and our force field. It is as if I am providing the vehicle for her to say goodbye to this place she so loved.

I remember this was the case with Kelly. During that last month of her life, Kelly and I had created this same force field. It was confirmed later it was this very vibration which enabled me to travel through the tunnel with Kelly and enabled Kelly to catapult into a new form.

And now I was experiencing the same phenomenon with Mom. I am often taken back by how much the experience with Kelly prepared me for this one with Mom.

I feel, as I travel down this familiar road in Tahoe, I have a headset attached to my ear and on the other side of it is Mom.

It once again shows me, just as I witnessed with Kelly, there is no separation.

If we neutralize the pain and walk through the fears of abandonment and grief, there is no loss.

Here in the midst of the pine trees and mountain air I once again learn there is no separation between above and below other than the separation we create out of fear and disillusionment.

We can indeed access our point of power through loss if we are able and willing to cope with the change. We can experience true connectedness if we are equipped to deal with the separateness and are willing to trust and believe.

I carried that feeling throughout my whole road trip.

CHAPTER THIRTY-FOUR:
TAKING TIME TO HEAL

I was very blessed in that I was able to take two weeks in Tahoe and just write. There were many enlightening moments while there. On the month's anniversary of Mom's passing, I experienced an especially illuminating meditation. I woke up that morning a little weepy. I kept replaying the events of that last day over in my head.

The fact that I slept for those five minutes when Mom actually passed still puzzled me. It didn't make sense. I was sitting out in the sun and all of a sudden I remembered that experience I had had with Kelly the day after we had helped her go to the other side. I thought to myself, "I really want to know what happened during that infamous five minutes!" I intellectually knew what had happened – but I wanted to see it – to experience it for myself.

I came back to my sister's cabin, lit a fire; opened my Akashic Records, Mom's Akashic Records and the records of our relationship. I set the stage, tuned into Mom and asked her to show me what had actually taken place.

The scene begins with my kissing Mom goodnight and telling her I love her. The minute I laid down in that bed I fell into a deep sleep. I then see Mom lifting out of her body. She turns to me in her spirit body, and, just as she had done so many times in our physical lives together, she calls my name. "Cathy… Cathy."

As I hear her with my spiritual ears, I too lift out of my body. I nod to her knowingly. There are no words. I reach my hand out to her, and together we merge into this stream of liquid light. We flow up to where we are met by her childhood friend, Jean.

(I had been told earlier that Jean was Mom's "exit" person.

Mom is delighted to see her. Jean takes one hand, and I take the other.

There is a short stairway. It reminds me of the stairway that used to extend from our cellar to the outside. The three of us climb the stairs and there, waiting for Mom, is her Band of Angels. They are familiar faces, her sisters, her mother, Dad's mother and several of her friends who had crossed over before her.

I let go of Mom's hand as she begins to greet each of her close ones. The Band of Support then guides Mom into the Coliseum Darlene had mentioned. Mom's eyes are filled with awe.

I see Dad. He and Mom embrace. He then comes over and stands by my side. I am elated to see him. He puts his arm around me and tells me how proud he is of me. We stand there and watch Mom as she is embraced by the many that have come to welcome her home.

Mom's Guardian Angel comes over to thank me. He kisses my forehead and tells me how grateful he is that I helped Mom come home. "Your love helped her remember. The love the two of you experienced together helped her get home."

A sense of fulfillment followed me out of the meditation. On the anniversary of Mom's passing, she had given me the missing piece. I now understood why I had fallen into such a deep slumber. Mom had been waiting for me to do so. She had been waiting for me to help her go to the other side.

When I shared this experience with Darlene, she confirmed this was indeed the case.

It is not that I did not grieve after that experience–or did not shed tears. It just felt different.

On the trip back to Nebraska I had many conversations with my own guardians. I had many conversations with Dad. I began to piece together how the vibration of love that Mom and I felt, and even Kelly and I had attained, had definitely changed my heart and my life.

It established a new context for serenity. As long as I stay connected to that experience of love I feel no fear. I am in a constant state of faith. And when a feeling does emerge which distracts me from that state I use the tools I have acquired to neutralize the emotions. It never fails to help me find my way back to peace.

EPILOGUE:

I do not know what you believe.
But when the time comes
and death or loss,
in one way or another,
knocks on your door,
I encourage you to trust
you can cope.
Seize the opportunity
to move beyond your fears.
Give yourself the experience
of expanded hope and faith.
Try not to be afraid.
Take a deep breath.
Trust you can cope.
Expect to be astonished.
Then get out of your own way
and receive.

SECTION THREE:
Backstage-with the Five Stages of Grief!

*I*n response to the impending loss of my pet named Kelly, my heart changed. By sustaining the desire to stay connected over a period of a month the actual vibration of my heart was altered. That next month my income quadrupled. I believe the vibration in my heart attracted abundance into every area of my life even though my attention was focused simply on the love I felt for my pet.

I had given every inner child the time needed to express what needed to be expressed and used the tapping techniques and sequences to neutralize all fears. I moved BEYOND COMPASSION- even beyond a reverence for what was happening. From that time on I did not respond to my world in the same way. I moved into a state of grace and acceptance I had never before experienced. Six months later I drew on these same tools to cope with the loss of my own Mother.

It has been an eight-month process. I cannot even imagine what my life will attract as I now return to it with an even deeper connection to this bliss.

My hope is that the stories shared and the exercises provided will offer you the same opportunities.

GENERAL THOUGHTS ON THE PROCESS OF GRIEF

To embrace grief as I did it is essential that you get comfortable with grief. To do so, it is useful to have a fuller understanding of grief because most cultures do not embrace grief. They support a more stoic approach to loss and encourage the " buck up and bear it," philosophy. In the long run, that approach does not work. That approach did not work when we were children, and it does not work when we confront loss as an adult. As children, however, we did not have a choice. We had to survive. We did not have the emotional maturity and capacity to process such intense emotions. But as we progress into adulthood we ideally develop more sophisticated coping mechanisms.

Unfortunately, this is not always the case. The degree of trauma experienced in childhood can thwart those efforts and, instead, we can get locked into a fight, flight, or freeze, response and spend much of our life bouncing amidst situations to which we react. The psychological community is now referring to this response to the world as a complex form of "post-traumatic stress disorder", or simply PTSD. We will discuss PTSD in more detail later. What is relevant for this grief overview is that when PTSD which originated in childhood is coupled with a major loss in adulthood, such as that of a loved one, the coping mechanisms of the past trauma will dictate the response to the current crisis at hand.

But even if we have not suffered from PTSD, most experience at least some residual childhood grief that has not been resolved. Research now suggests that the essential wound we encounter the first time we experience the world as unsafe establishes the blueprint with which we will deal with loss throughout our lives. The context and intensity of our unresolved loss may differ. However, the commonality is that the lack of resolution is based on the conscious or unconscious fear that we will not be able to cope if we confront the depth of intense feeling associated with loss. What few realize, and what most cultures do not support, is the fact that *learning to embrace* the process of grief is *the antidote for* our fear that we will be unable to cope. Learning how to process grief is the most promising way to live a fulfilling life because it enables us to truly live life without fear.

Most of us are familiar with grief. We have experienced loss. We relate to grief as a process that must be endured, but only when there is a *major* loss, a measurable loss, one that has a beginning and an end. Grief, however, is a predictable process we experience on a regular basis in response to the many challenges we face each day. These commonly accepted stages of grief are experienced in response to even the little moments of loss–minute losses–like the momentary loss of self-esteem we feel when we do not live up to our own potential, or the loss of trust we might feel when a friend does not live up to our expectations. Without realizing it, we progress through the five predictable stages of grief even in response to these minor infractions.

Often, the process takes as little as ten minutes. But irrespective of how long it takes, we do progress through the same stages of feelings one experiences when confronted with a major loss. We feel anxious, (stage one-denial, panic, anxiety) which is mitigated by a desire to fix or alter the situation, (stage two-bargaining). When this fails, we feel anger and irritation, (stage three-anger). When we are exhausted by our anger, we begin to let go. We collapse into the truth of the loss and feel the deep despair, (stage four-despair). If we are lucky, with time, we do resign ourselves to the loss. We accept the loss. And, depending on the severity of the loss, we do reinvest and move on, (stage five-acceptance and resolution).

But some are not that lucky. An individual can get stuck in any one of these five stages of grief. If one's PTS is triggered, he or she can ruminate about the situation for days. If this occurs then, irrespective of the nature of the loss, the individual will continue to get retriggered at the stage of grief he or she was unable to resolve in the first place. This person simply goes from one triggering experience to the next, forever caught in a state or reactivity, experiencing few moments of peace and calm. Anxiety-ridden and overly active in co-dependent behavior, he or she can approach the world with rage and anger or suffer from depression and despair.

Nonetheless, whether our childhood trauma was severe or not, most of us find we are living in a society in which unresolved grief has become an epidemic. The current economic situation continued threats of terrorism, and relentless wars coupled with current stresses of daily life leave us afraid and confused—triggering childhood wounds and adult doubts about our ability to cope. We are thrown into the stages of grief as we express our unresolved anxiety, confusion, fear, anger, and sadness, through compulsive and addictive behaviors.

We may eat too much; drink, drug or smoke too much; love, shop, work, gamble or worry too much. We live out of fear rather than faith—compulsion rather than choice—isolation rather than unity, as we long to feel safe and secure. But there is little human security. Whatever excessive behavior we choose, it simply serves to numb the insecurity of the unknown, the pain of our grief.

Millions are pharmaceutically treated for depression, anxiety disorders, and post-traumatic stress. Each of these ailments has its roots in unresolved grief. When our grief is not processed, the lingering feelings of loss accumulate. They erode our hope, lead to rage and despair. When faced with a major loss, these unresolved feelings roar deep within and exacerbate the current crisis. The depth of emotion can become a source of fear–fear that we will not cope.

And there is some truth to this possibility. The underlying affects of our grief get stored in our body, morph into physical ailments, and become a steady source of emotional, physical, mental, and spiritual, decline. The emotions may get numbed by our addictions, but our grief does not go away. It lays dormant, threatening to resurface with a vengeance, demanding the attention it deserves.

Why is grief deserving? It is deserving because these five stages of emotion are a natural response to living our life fully. It is deserving because dealing with the contrast and the resolution of that contrast is what invites our soul to grow. Contrast is what we experience when, in response to challenging emotions, we restrict and contract. But that very contraction shows us where we are out alignment with something in our life. We are out of alignment with our higher self, our most illuminated self. Every challenging emotion we encounter can be categorized as one of these five stages of grief. And every contrasting feeling, when resolved, holds the opportunity for expansion and growth.

When we experience loss, it is indicative of our attachment to someone or something. The attachment itself can be healthy and fluid… the resolution of its loss expanding and illuminating. When we lose someone we love, or lose something of great value, our feelings of grief are a testament to how much that someone or something truly meant to us. It is a sign that we allowed ourselves to love, to be attached, to care. To grieve is to be alive. Grieving is a way we let go and allow a new form of the relationship or situation to emerge. That is the promise of the fifth stage of grief. We accept the loss of what was. We open up for a new form of connection to unfold and take its place.

As I look back on the experiences I had with Kelly, with Mom, and truly, with all of the moments of grief I have felt during this lifetime, I feel a sense of fulfillment. Being able to breathe through the grief and get to the place where I felt such completion enabled me to stay connected to my Creator, to my inner being, my higher self. That connection enabled me to get out of my way and let the situation of loss morph into its next evolution. Trusting the process of grief empowered me to love without fear. That trust is what enabled me to stay connected to those I lost, before, and after, their passing, in the profound ways evident in the pages before this. My life is richer because I do not fear love. It is richer because I do not fear emotion. Again, to love means to live, to live means to experience loss. If we are afraid of loss, we are afraid to live.

When you can stay connected to your spiritual source, ask for, and receive insight regarding the higher purpose of even your momentary losses, and fearlessly embrace the process of grief, you can rest assured you will be able to successfully live life unafraid to love. You will re-establish your trust in being able to cope. You will come to have faith in your ability to breathe through the anxiety, embrace the momentary anger, disillusionment, and despair, return to a state of resolution and trust that accompanies your daily losses. When you can grieve, you can live life without hesitation. When you can grieve, you can love without fear. You can nestle safely in the comfort of the arms of your Higher Power and feel bigger than your fears.

It is said there are two predominant states of emotion–love and fear. We are either feeling afraid or feeling love. Every other emotion falls somewhere in between. We cannot feel love and fear at the same time.

What can you do when you slip from the safety and comfort of trusting your Higher Power into the depths of fear that you will not survive? You guessed it! You can embrace the process of grief.

But to embrace grief, you have to understand grief in a more practical and non-intimidating way. Before you can truly relate to my story, and attempt to process your feelings in a similar manner, it is important to understand that **you are already in a constant state of grief.** As has already been suggested, whether identified as such or not, you are already processing through these stages in response to the events of your daily life.

Let me give you a simple example. Although you might not realize it you experience the five stages of grief every time you miss a phone call–well at least every time you miss a phone call you wanted to receive. Picture for a moment those times you've heard your cell phone ring but could not get to it in time. You hurriedly dropped what you were doing but to no avail. You got there too late. The caller had hung up.

What was your response?

Whether identified as such or not, it was most often the first stage of grief. Denial… followed by tension and anxiety related to what you perceive you have missed. You may find yourself pushing 'call back,' but to no avail. The caller is leaving you a message or has gone on to another call. What happens then? You feel frustrated. You try to manage the situation by calling again. And this cat and mouse game can go on for several minutes.

Have you ever talked to your phone as if you are talking to the person trying to reach you? "Pick up! Pick Up," you command. In today's world, you most likely send a text the message commanding a response. That's when you slip into the second stage of grief–bargaining with the dead phone as you hear yourself plea,"Just, pick up! I'm here–just callback!" But inevitably the other person has shut off the phone, or is engaged and cannot connect. What do you feel when "managing the situation" does not work? Most often you experience anger and disappointment, and sometimes sadness and despair.

The feelings may be mild. But they are the feelings of grief nonetheless. The sadness does give way to the knowledge that the person will indeed call back, or the call comes through and you breathe a sigh of relief for the need has been met. However, you come to terms with this incident; a resolution does ensue.

You first experienced disbelief that you had missed the call. This disbelief covered up the initial anxiety which got denied as you tried to manage the situation. When this did not work, you most likely felt irritation or even anger, which then gave way to despair, And then, ultimately, you resigned yourself to the fact that the person would indeed call back. In a period of several minutes, you experienced the five stages of grief. If you recognize these steps, you move through them and do not get stuck. The more you befriend this process, the more moments of contentment you will have.

So I encourage you to have the courage to befriend this process. Learn as much from this material as you can, then seize the opportunity of your loss to learn more elsewhere. Relate to grief as a way to manage and resolve all of life's challenges and disappointments. Don't deny it. Treat grief as a friend. Learn how to breathe through your anxiety, let go, and give up your attempts to control the outcomes of situations over which you have no control. Give yourself permission to beat on a pillow, scream in the mirror, or throw a tantrum in the safety of your own home as you rid yourself of the energy of your anger. Learn how to befriend the void and emptiness of your despair, so that place within you can be cleansed and prepared for you to bring in something new. Find that serene point of reference then make that your goal to constantly process whatever keeps you from sustaining that sense of calm and peace.

Experience life-stay present for life-by identifying the stages of grief. Your comfort with grief is a sign that you are not afraid to live. It is a sign you have the courage to love. if you are willing to actively engage in the process of grief, if you know how to graciously move through those stages, you will have a method by which you can deal with whatever life hands you.And life does hand you challenges. It hands us all challenges.

Part of the human experience is to bump up against the glitches in our daily life. **No matter how good we are**, we are going to have to deal with life's challenges. You are going to get stuck in traffic jams. Friends are going to disappoint you. Things are not going to turn out as you had hoped. You are going to get hooked into old family roles or simply have "bad days." But if you can become comfortable with the process of grief, you can live fearlessly with the assurance that you will indeed be able to cope. If you can cope, you can love and live from your heart. If you can cope, you can succeed! And one of the most profound tools to assist you in coping is the new energy therapy most commonly referred to as EFT which is short for *"Emotional Freedom Techniques"*!

EMOTIONAL FREEDOM TECHNIQUES – GARY CRAIG'S EFT

As you have witnessed, the main ingredient in dealing with the feelings of grief is having the capacity to cope with them. One of the most effective ways to do this is to neutralize them with a self-administered form of acupressure called energy tapping. I am a big fan of tapping. Tapping is what gave me a viable method to move through the gut-wrenching emotions of loss I faced. So before we explore the stages of grief related to the losses of your present and your past, I want to introduce you to energy tapping. This introduction will give you an idea of how you can apply this technique to augment your ability to cope.

I will also provide you with a worksheet on how to design your own tapping sequences so you can begin to befriend this process yourself. However, never be afraid to seek professional guidance. Grief can be treacherous. You sometimes will need a guide.

Please note–the the following overview of traditional tapping is paraphrased from Gary Craig's EFT Web Site which is www.emofree.com

Energy Tapping, commonly referred to as Emotional Freedom Techniques (EFT) by Gary Craig, is based on a discovery that has provided thousands with relief from pain, addictions, diseases, and emotional issues. Simply stated, it is an emotional version of acupuncture except needles aren't necessary. Instead, you stimulate well-established energy meridian points on your body by tapping on them with your fingertips. The process is easy to memorize and is portable so you can do it anywhere. The process launches off the EFT Discovery Statement which says...

> ***"The cause of all negative emotions is***
> ***a disruption in the body's energy system."***

The common sense approach of EFT draws its power from two sources. The time-honored Eastern discoveries that have been around for over 5,000 years and Albert Einstein, who told us back in the 1920's that everything, including our bodies, is composed of energy. These two sources and ideas have been largely ignored by Western Healing Practices, and that is why Energy Tapping often works where nothing else will. Emotions are energy and can, therefore, be managed by working with the energy systems in one's body.

WHAT EXACTLY DOES ENERGY TAPPING DO?

Tapping on prescribed points sends an electrical impulse to the electrical energy system of your body which is being affected by the feelings of loss. When you simultaneously stimulate the meridian points while stating phrases which represent your current discomfort, you "neutralize" the energy associated with that emotion. Tapping addresses every feeling you experience when facing a loss. It essentially unties the knot of your tension and enables you to experience a state of calm and peace. Once the tension is released the system affected can relax, and energy can more effectively flow through your entire body.

THE PROCEDURE

EFT process begins with three setup phrases. I use the setup phrases to identify the ambivalence and contrasting feelings of any issue. When I speak of the contrast of feelings, I am referring to the conflicting feelings you experience with respect to the part of you who holds the pain around the loss (usually a younger part of self) and the part of you who is spiritually and psychologically advanced enough to be able to respond to the pain. This interaction between the wounded, grief-stricken part of you and the healer within you is the agent of the resolution of your grief.

In the focus questions provided before each stage of grief, you will be able to identify the belief systems and patterns of the younger part of you which impact your ability to experience that respective stage of grief. Your adult self obviously grieves as well—but the resolution of your grief usually involves dealing with the residual impact of your grief which has been triggered by the current loss.

Each setup phrase positions a challenging feeling with a more positive affirmation. Sometimes, as in traditional tapping, the dichotomous statements are symptom-related. In interactional tapping, ™ the contrasting feelings are those of the younger self who is more traumatized, and the healthier part of you who can cope, and can therefore, comfort and support

The tapping procedure itself is divided into three sections. You first *neutralize the negative* thoughts and feelings, then introduce the *possibility of change,* and finish with a strong infusion of your *conviction to change. Sometimes this is done in three segments. Sometimes the second and third segments are merged together to create more of a flow between the two.*

PLEASE NOTE: You begin the sequence with three setup statements which you state while tapping on the karate chop. Called a psychological reversal, the wording combines a statement about the problem with a

statement of affirmation accepting the problem. This combination prepares your psyche and body to accept the energetic correction of this imbalance.

THE TAPPING POINTS

I have provided a graphic which illustrates the places upon you will want to tap. It takes only a few rounds to get the hang of the sequences, but until your feel comfortable with the procedure, this graphic will be a nice reminder.

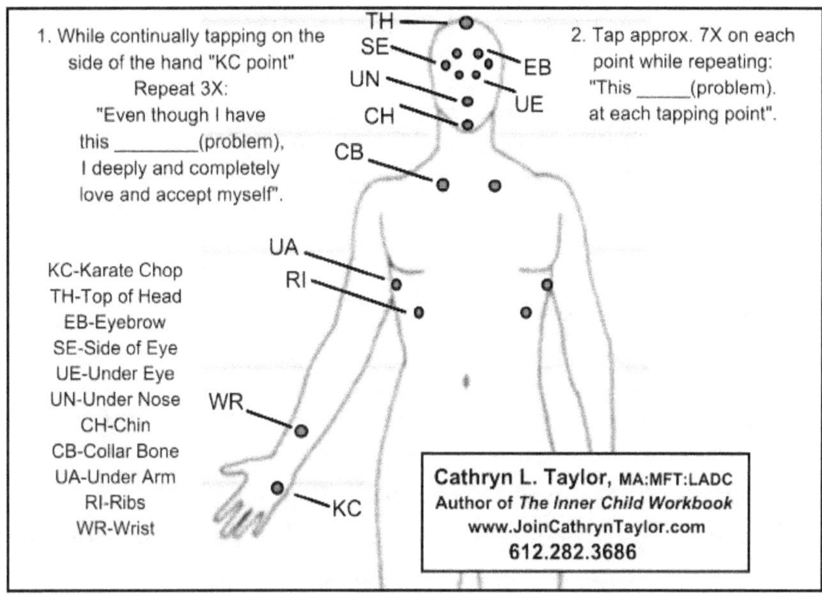

Again, just to reiterate, traditional energy tapping targets the symptoms of your grief. My signature method of interactive tapping™ addresses the symptoms from a relationship perspective. In other words, I focus on the interaction between the part of you who is experiencing the emotions of loss, and the healer within you who can respond. It is this interactive tapping™ that facilitates such profound healing.

During my crisis, I found both approaches had merit. Before I could neutralize the challenging emotions of the younger parts of me, who had gotten triggered in response to impending loss of Mom and Kelly, I used the traditional tapping methods to address my immediate gut-wrenching reactions. As you witnessed in my story–if I was raw with emotion I did traditional tapping–if I had identified the emotions as being those of a younger part of me and needed to externalize a more emotionally distraught part of me–then I used my style of "relationship" tapping. I cleared my adult self so that part of me could ultimately deal with the more provocative feelings of the younger self who had collapsed into the unresolved grief from my past.

In fact, before we begin this process I want to guide you through the simple procedure of clearing your adult self. That way, if, during the exercises on each respective stage, you do begin to feel a strong emotion you will be equipped with a way to respond. Please refer to the graphic of the tapping points. The sequences for clearing your adult self follow.

EXERCISE: TAPPING SEQUENCE TO CLEAR THE ADULT SELF

Begin by continuously tapping on the karate point while stating the following:

Even though there may be some things I am not totally in harmony with today, I choose, for this time, to suspend those feelings so I can now focus entirely on being present for this inner work.

So even though I may need to neutralize some general irritations, I am going to do that now because I am committed to clearing this up so I can be present for this work.

So even though I may not be in total harmony, I am willing to suspend any feelings that may distract me right now so I can be clear and open enough to be present for this work.

Next, you will do the general neutralizing. It involves stating reminder phrases while you tap on the designated end points.

NEUTRALIZING THE NEGATIVE: *REFER TO GRAPHIC AS NEEDED.*

Corner of the Eyebrow: *Generally disturbed… A little bit antsy… Clear out any anger.*

Side of Eye: *Clear out all distraction.*

Under Eye: *Any frustration.*

Upper lip: *A little bit fatigued.*

Under the lip: *But choose to feel empowered to do this work.*

Collarbone: *Am excited to show up for this work.*

Under Arm: *Have committed to showing up to do this work.*

Chest Bone: *I feel empowered to respond—I am ready to be present and to begin to do this work.*

Wrist: *I ask my Higher Guidance to assist…*

Top of Head: *… so that I can move forward and clear this disturbance and heal.*

***These statements are just a sample of how you would neutralize anything that is current in your day-to-day life.* Continue to tap on each of the end points until you move through any resistance to being present to address the feelings which need to be embraced.**

This tapping sequence provides the opportunity for you to step into the vibration of a healthy, adult self. The next step is to construct a strong connection between this adult self and your higher self. Obtaining and sustaining a spiritual connection while confronting these stages of grief is necessary. It gives your loss a purpose and helps you move from being a victim to your loss to being a student of your loss. It is this relationship that will enable you to embrace these stages of grief with the courage and confidence you will be able to cope.

Building A Bridge Between Your Adult Self And Spiritual Self

This bridging can only occur when you are ready to participate in your own healing because it requires your willingness to become an "active participant" in the healing process. As you have progressed in your adult life, you have had experiences that have strengthened your ability to deal with the world. But some losses are above and beyond those normal experiences. Loss often needs a spiritual context. That context takes place when you form a partnership between your adult self and your higher self. Some call this self their "inner being," the "higher self," the "spiritual self." It doesn't matter what you call that expanded part of you. What is relevant is that you find a way to develop a partnership between these two parts of you.

Interactive Tapping™ fosters this partnership. My interactive brand of tapping is built on the principle that, as an adult, you have acquired the skills to respond in a protective and nurturing manner. If this is not the case, then it would be useful to find role models that you can emulate so you can "act as if" you have a nurturing voice until you develop the ability to use the self-soothing language that can quiet the feelings of unrest. "Acting as if" (pretending you are someone else who is compassionate and accepting) is a way your inner adult learns how to respond in a way which invites trust. Partnering with the higher self teaches you how to raise your vibration to the point where you can experience compassion and acceptance for the more fragile parts that may not be quite as mature and able to cope.

Breathing is the primary method that enables you to merge with this higher, more peaceful and compassionate, part of self. Every time you breathe in you have the opportunity to fill yourself with the energy of the Universe. Every time you exhale, you are invited to release your tension and your fear. Inhaling expands your vibrational frequency so you can more easily merge with your Higher Self which ensures more ability to cope. Therefore, breathing is where we will begin.

EXERCISE: THE CHAKRA/BREATH EXERCISE

In this first exercise, your breathing awakens the energy centers of your body called chakras. Each of us has seven primary energy centers which connect our spiritual body to our physical one. They operate on subtle levels and are invisible to the naked eye, yet affect every aspect of our life. In effect, these seven centers act as transformers—or sending and receiving stations—negotiating the flow of energy which comes from us and to us moment to moment. They are situated in the etheric fields of our being along the spinal column at the base of the spine, the pelvic area, midway between the base and the navel, near the heart, throat, and brow or "third eye" area and at the top of the head.

These chakras are the central processing centers for every aspect of our being. The blockage we carry into adulthood from the losses we encountered in childhood will show up as energetic dysfunctions in the chakras. These, in turn, usually give rise to disorders in the body. These blockages disrupt how we think, feel, and connect, with our Higher Guidance and authentic self. A defect in the energy flow through any given chakra will impair the entire energy field's ability to process energy—affecting all levels of the being. Our energy field is a holistic entity; every part of it affects every other part.

Tapping and clearing our chakra system connects our physical self with our non-physical self. It constructs this necessary bridge. In this exercise, you will be guided to gently tap on each of the correlating centers in your physical form. The diagram on the following page shows you where to tap. This tapping is done with your open hand. You just gently tap on each area of your body as if you were bouncing a small ball. This tapping sequence was inspired by EFT Master Carol Tuttle www.caroltuttle.com/. The procedure connects you to your authentic self and strengthens the partnership which enables you to better neutralize and release the strong emotions of your grief. To begin, refer to the graphic on the next page for guidance. Simply tap gently on the designated location of each energy center, again, as if you were bouncing a small ball while you simultaneously state the words associated with clearing each chakra. This exercise will get your energy flowing in the right direction. Start with the root chakra (or first chakra) and move up.

7th Chakra-God Center-State while you tap-*I am now willing to align myself with my authentic self, to connect with integrity, honesty, and trust.*

6th Chakra-higher vision center-State while you tap-*I am now willing to see through the eyes of my authentic self-to open the door to my intuition with the confidence and certainty that I am connected with my higher truth and am committed to attracting my highest desires.*

5th Chakra-truth center-State while you tap-*I am now willing to release and let go of all reluctance to speak what I know. I am willing to speak my truth with integrity, accountability, and trust. I am willing to receive all that I deserve.*

4th Chakra-heart center-State while you tap-*I am now willing to open my heart to unconditional love so I can experience the true connection between my spiritual and physical selves.*

3rd Chakra-the power center-State while you tap-*I am willing to allow myself the feeling of empowerment-to release all attachment to feeling like a victim and instead allow myself to experience the feeling of expansion and empowerment.*

2nd Chakra-the pleasure center-State while you tap-*I am*

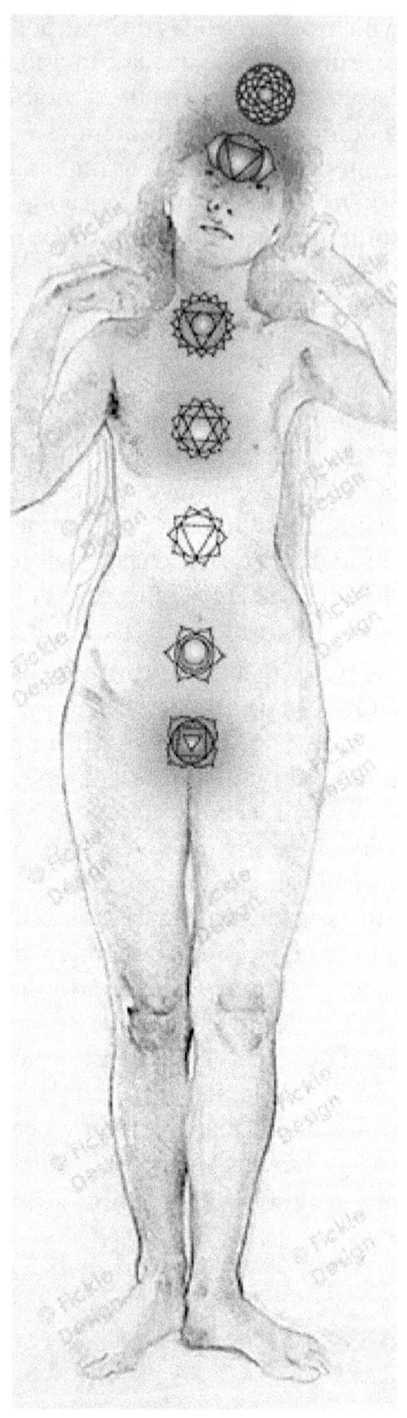

willing to have faith in myself and my ability to discern–to set the limits and boundaries that allow me to connect with my authentic self.

[1st] Chakra–root chakra–the center of connection and safety and trust–State while you tap–*I am willing to feel safe enough to trust and connect.*

Now that you have bridged between your higher self and your adult self you can work with the exercises and tapping sequences that will help you resolve your grief–the grief of your present loss and, ultimately, the grief retriggered from your past as well.

Exploring The Five Stages Of Grief Related To Your Current Loss

If you have just recently experienced the loss of someone you love, then you are most likely feeling relief to learn that your grief is the natural response to the loss you are feeling, that your grief will progress in relatively a predictable manner and that this structure usually follows five distinct stages. Knowing grief has a structure makes the process feel a little more manageable. And although these stages do not always progress sequentially, you will most likely relate to each of these stages–all of which will be present in the process of your grief.

A Few General Instructions: Each stage of grief you address targets the current feelings associated with your recent loss. However, the exercises will also inspire and prepare you to ultimately deal with the unresolved loss retriggered from your past. Below are a few general instructions that will further explain the structure of this work.

1.   *There are a series of journal questions which will help you clarify your personal response to each stage. This inquiry will help you begin to differentiate between your adult self who is now experiencing the grief and your inner child whose residual grief may have been triggered. The tapping in this next section will primarily address your current experience. In the section that follows you*

will be given the directions and information needed for processing the grief of your inner child.

2. *I suggest you have a journal you can use specifically for the purpose of recording your responses. It is nice to have your discoveries and reactions contained in one folder. This folder organizes your grief in a way that, again, makes the process seem more manageable.*

3. *Specific exercises aimed to identify your personal response to your loss provide the focus for your tapping sequences that are offered for each stage. Tapping is the method by which your grief is resolved, but your inquiries and exploration provide the content needed to make the tapping efficient. Exploring your reaction to each stage in this fashion, before you engage in the tapping exercises, provides your psyche with the meta-levels of emotion that will be neutralized and released as you tap on the respective end points of the electrical circuitry in your body.*

4. *The procedure of tapping, as has been explained, sends the electrical impulse through your body that effectively relaxes the energetic disturbance stimulated by your personal reaction to each stage of your grief. The more active that energetic disturbance is, in other words, the more you have dislodged the feelings that have been repressed, the more accessible they will be to the actual healing that energy tapping provides.*

5. *Additional instructions will be provided at each stage and are self-explanatory.*

STAGE ONE: PANIC–DENIAL–ANXIETY

DISCUSSION–Our first response to loss is panic. We go into the fight or flight response. We shut down, deny, go into a state of shock, (called psychic numbing). We want to deny the truth of the loss. To embrace it leaves us feeling too raw. The anxiety is the tension we feel in the pit of our stomach when we try to imagine life without our loved one. It is that response to feeling something has been ripped from our very core. We get panic-stricken. We can even experience a psychological split because we cannot endure the pain–some get aggressive and hostile, others become depressed.

And of course, there is always the option to compulsively or addictively act out. As was discussed in the previous section, medicating our grief quiets the tumultuous feelings, sometimes for decades. We lose sight as to what the panic is even related. We simply experience a restlessness quieted by our drug or destructive behavior. Eventually, we either die of the addiction or find ourselves in recovery. If we make it into recovery, the unresolved loss is waiting for us. We begin the journey through the stages of grief–the bargaining, anger, and despair. But now there is the grief of the time lost as we ran from our grief. Those feelings also need to be addressed and processed if we are to ever come to a resolution.

FOCUS QUESTIONS–To prepare for your EFT sequences respond to the following questions and record your responses in your journal.

1. *How have you dealt with the anxiety regarding the given situation upon which you now want to focus?*

2. *Have you channeled your energy from your loss into work? Did you deflect to another person, or activity, or just implode and become riddled with depression–perhaps consumed with shame and guilt over your regrets.*

3. *Did you numb out with your addictions–do you excessively eat, smoke, or exercise… compulsively spend or gamble?*

4. *If so, how long ago was the actual loss that you now need to address?*

5. *Take a moment to really ponder how you have dealt with your tension and anxiety… how you have avoided the feelings you felt you could not bear.*

6. *Bring your focus back to that moment when you first heard about this loss–notice how you managed the anxiety which accompanied this gut-wrenching experience. Notice where in your body you held your anxiety?*

7. *Record your thoughts and feelings in your journal.*

SUGGESTED EXERCISE–You might want to further your exploration by drawing a picture of your anxiety. Look at this picture when doing your EFT rounds. Customize the reminder phrases to match the feelings your picture provokes. The setup phrases establish the context of your anxiety and identify the emotion or state of mind you are trying to attain. They state that even though you are experiencing a negative emotion, you accept yourself nonetheless. The setup phrases can also identify what it is you currently feel about your situation and what you want to feel. The reminder phrases then assist you in addressing the challenging emotions as you introduce the possibility of feeling something new which morphs into your conviction to embrace the feelings of this stage of grief.

If you need a reminder of where to tap refer to the graphic in the previous section which illustrated the tapping points. While tapping on your karate end point state each of the following setup statements three times.

Even though I felt anxious in this situation–,I can feel it in the pit of my stomach, or the back of my neck, or in the stress, I hold in my shoulders–I love myself fully and completely.

Even though I feel great anxiety on my recent loss, I now choose to work with this fear, release it from my body, so I can begin to resolve this grief.

Even though I am experiencing great anxiety about this loss, I choose to believe I am in the arms of my Higher Power and, with that support, I choose to begin to let go.

Now begin your tapping rounds. Tap on each of the end points 5 to 6 times as you state the phrases listed. Again, use these statements as a guide, but feel free to customize your statements using your own words. Do as many rounds as it takes to experience a release. Once you reach that point, let it be for right now. Allow that process to settle into your psyche. You will know when it is time to resume your grieving process. Remember, one of the goals of processing your grief is to return to a state of trust for yourself. That means trusting your own pacing as well.

NEUTRALIZING THE NEGATIVE

Side of the eye: *Really feel anxious… feel it in my stomach, shoulders or neck…*

Corner of the eye: *Cannot imagine surviving this loss…*

Under the eye: *This loss really frightens me…*

Upper lip: *Am afraid I won't survive…*

Lower lip: *What if I don't survive…*

Collarbone: *So frightened I won't survive…*

Under the arm: *Just want this fear to go away… want it out of my body and soul…*

Chest bone: *So afraid to move on… to forget… to be alone…*

Head: *Just want this fear to be gone… gone out of my body and soul.*

Moving from the Possibility of Change to Conviction…

Side of the eye: *Maybe if I bury myself in the arms of my Higher Power…*

Corner of the eye: *Maybe I can let go and let God…*

Under the eye: *Please Higher Power fill this void…*

Upper lip: *Help me move beyond this gut-wrenching loss and fear…*

Lower lip: *Just want to feel safe and believe I can cope…*

Collarbone: *Maybe with help, I can survive…*

Under the arm: *I choose now to turn this over…*

Chest bone: *I choose to surrender to my Higher Power and God…*

Head: *I am strong enough… I can survive. With help, I can survive this loss.*

Keep doing rounds until you can transmute this anxiety and can feel relaxed and calm at least at the moment. If you find you just cannot get there and you have already gone into the mode of trying to control, change, or fix, the situation, then proceed to work the bargaining stage of grief.

STAGE TWO: BARGAINING

DISCUSSION: When we can no longer tolerate the rawness of the loss we try to regain some sense of control by focusing on how we can change or fix the circumstances. Even though our attempts fail, the activity allows us to discharge some of the energy which gets stuck. These attempts are called the bargaining phase because we start making agreements with our self and with the loss of someone or something without which we feel will not survive. If we are dealing with the end-of-life transition, we try to bargain with the circumstances of the ending. In a frantic manner, we try to manage the situation to ward off the inevitable pain.

FOCUS QUESTIONS–To prepare for your EFT sequences respond to the following questions in your journal.

1. *How did you try to make this situation better?*

2. *What did you do behaviorally to try to change this situation or ignore this situation to pretend it did not exist?*

3. *This was your attempt to bargain with these circumstances. Did it work? If not, did you try something else or did you collapse into your anger or despair?*

4. *Is there anything about which you feel regret? If so, try to describe the circumstances and the accompanying feelings. This belief that it could be your fault can be the source of much of your grief. It is important to flush those feelings out and address them.*

SUGGESTED EXERCISE–If it feels useful to do so explore the deeper meaning of your attempts to manage the loss. Determine who inside feels such a need to change this situation. Who finds your present circumstances so intolerable? What motivates you to change, fix, or control, this situation in your adult world can be entirely different that what motivated you as a child to manage the loss felt at not being safe. If you separate these two motivations and focus now on the adult's need to bargain the neutralization process will be more effective. The inner child's feelings need to bargain and control will be addressed in the next section.

Tap continually on your karate point as you state each of the following setup statements three times. Customize these to fit your needs.

Even though I tried but failed to control, fix, or change this situation (imagine it in your mind's eye) I love myself fully and completely.

Even though I have put great effort into changing this situation to no avail, and have exhausted myself in my attempts, I love myself fully and completely and am willing to neutralize this need to control.

Even though I have tried so very hard, I now realize I could not have altered this situation, and I love myself enough to accept this fact and detach from all regret.

Use the following samples to begin your neutralization process. Add your own phrases accordingly, but continue to tap around the end points stating your reminder phrases until you have neutralized the negative, introduced the possibility of change, and feel a conviction regarding your new stance.

Neutralizing the Negative...

Side of the eye: *Really tried so very hard...*

Corner of the eye: *Was so exhausted with my attempts...*

Under the eye: *Just wish I could now let it go...*

Upper lip: *But fight this regret I could not fix the situation...*

Lower lip: *It is so in my nature to jump in...*

Collarbone: *I just need let go of any regret and give it to God...*

Under the arm: *But this regret...*

Chest bone: *I just don't seem to be able to let it go...*

Head: *Wish I could relax, let go and give it to God.*

Moving from the Possibility of Change to Conviction...

Side of the eye: *Maybe I did the best that I could...*

Corner of the eye: *Maybe I can tap instead of reacting...*

Under the eye: *Maybe what I can change is the way I respond...*

Upper lip: *Maybe I don't always have to be the one…*
Lower lip: *I am going to tap until I can let go…*
Collarbone: *Tap myself through this regret and shame…*
Under the arm: *Shame I could not change the outcome…*
Chest bone: *Shame I could not fix the situation…*
Head: *I feel strong and secure in my ability to let go!*

Hopefully, this tapping sequence empowers you to make peace with all that you could not control. Nonetheless, you will still feel anger that you have to move on without your loved one. You may have resolved your anger at yourself because you could not alter the situation. But there may still be anger that you have to live without the one you loved. And as you will see, that anger is an essential ingredient to your truly moving on. Accepting the loss as it will be imperative if you are to be open to the new form that can evolve.

STAGE THREE – A N G E R

Anger seeps in once we realize our bargaining is not going to work or we simply feel angry and agitated at the loss of our cherished object–be it a person or a situation. This is often expressed as crankiness or being critical of everything around us. The irritation enables us to discharge some of the energy of the anger but keeps us from totally letting go of an attachment that can no longer exist.

But part of us does not want to let go. We feel angry that we even have to let go. We do not want to feel the loss. Often our anger is covert and even misdirected. It may be expressed at our self for blowing it. *"It's not nice to be angry."* We can feel shame or guilt for feeling angry. On the other hand, we may project our anger onto another–blaming that person for everything under the sun. Either way, the anger is not resolved. This criticalness or complaining does reduce the tension, but it does so without ever actually severing the tie to that which we lost. The transition from our blame/shame frame of mine occurs when we can no longer suppress it, and our feelings seep out in rage.

This rage is often raw and unfiltered. It fuels our courage, whether willingly or unwillingly, to embrace the depth of grief which accompanies our loss. Sometimes it is done with great volume because we don't know how to speak it without volume.

However, when we can truly, and honestly, embrace our anger, the volume diminishes. We speak our truth authentically and with great sadness. We admit how angry we are at our loss. The anger ultimately severs the hope that we can alter the reality of the loss. This collapse brings relief. We are finally free to stand in the void of the emptiness left by our loss as we collapse into the next stage of grief, the sadness, and the despair.

But before you are ready to entertain that relief you need to experience your anger and neutralize the attachment which is held in place by your anger. The following will assist you in that process.

FOCUS QUESTIONS: To prepare for your EFT sequences respond to the following questions in your journal.

1. *Take a moment to think about your loss. Determine when and how you experience or have experienced, the irritation or anger of this stage of your grief.*

2. *Do, or did, you recall feeling irritated at anything/everything around you? If so, that is covert anger.*

3. *Do, or did, you feel righteous–vindictive–aggressive? This is an expression of overt anger–misdirected anger.*

4. *Do, or did, you have a shorter temper with others–with yourself–with circumstances in your life? This is an example of generalized anger?*

5. *Do, or did, you feel like you wanted revenge–like you wanted to pay the person back and get even… reject them? If so, if it feels safe, use the following exercises and tapping sequences to revisit that rage and anger now–revenge anger.*

Suggested Exercise– *Use words or images and describe your feelings. Record all of the feelings you have identified then bring your focus to that rage and anger as you state the setup phrases that enable you to accept right where you are with your rage.*

Begin by tapping continuously on the karate chop point.

Even though I felt/feel rage (anger, revenge, etc.) in this situation (imagine it in your mind's eye), I love myself fully and completely."

Even though I am really angry I have to go on without the one I love; I want to accept this transition with ease.

So even though this is devastating to feel this loss, and I am so angry I have to endure without _____________ (name the person or thing) in my life, I want to embrace these feelings of rage. I want to feel these feelings so I can begin to let go… so I can sever this hope and feel the void.

Tap on the end points 5 to 6 times while you state your reminder phrases. Use the ones below but make up your own until you sense you have truly exhausted your anger and you are ready to consider moving on.

Neutralizing the Negative…

Side of the eye: *But I don't want to let go.*

Corner of the eye: *This really is not fair.*

Under the eye: *Why did this have to happen?*

Upper lip: *I was not ready for this. I should not have to deal with this.*

Lower lip: *I am so angry!*

Collarbone: *I don't want to be alone.*

Under the arm: *I should not have to be alone?*

Chest bone: *I am so angry!*

Head: *I will never let go.*

Moving from the Possibility of Change to Conviction–*When ready continue with the next phase of your tapping as you move into the possibility of letting go and moving on.*

Side of the eye: *But is it good for me to hang on?*

Corner of the eye: *I hate that I have to let go.*

Under the eye: *Who will I be if I let go?*

Upper lip: *I have lost the object of my love.*

Lower lip: __________ (*name of the person, loved one or object of your loss*) *is gone.*

Collarbone: *God, how it hurts.*

Under the arm: *But maybe it is time to release and let go.*

Chest bone: *Am I ready to admit this loss?*

Head: *Can I really survive if I let go?*

Another Round…

Side of the eye: *God, am I ready to speak my truth?*

Corner of the eye: *Can I really survive and be this raw.*

Under the eye: *I hate going on without* __________________ (*Name the object of your loss*)

Upper lip: *The truth is I don't want to be on this earth alone!*

Lower lip: *But I am alone, and it hurts!*

Collarbone: *It really, really hurts.*

Under the arm: *I hate being alone.*

Chest bone: *It pisses me off that I have to deal with this.*

Head: *I don't know how I will ever go on without* __________________ (*name the person or object of your love*) *without him/her or it.*

Again, continue tapping until you feel you have truly embraced the energy of your anger. Remember, this is the force that will let you move on and allow the new form of this relationship to unfold. When you speak your truth, you free yourself of the denial that your loved one is gone.

STAGE FOUR–DESPAIR–After allowing the severing of your hope there is usually an exhaustion–an emotional and physical exhaustion. It takes energy to hold on to those feelings of loss. Despair over this situation can feel like complete hopelessness–sadness–numbness. Despair is that experience of apathy and of giving up which leads to a sense of surrender. But most often the surrender begins with that apathy of complete hopelessness.

You will feel tired and worn out. You will need to sleep a great deal and let the reality of this loss settle into your psyche. You are readjusting to life without this object of your love. Many mistake despair for depression. In reality, it is the exact opposite. Although the two feeling states feel the same their function is quite different.

Depression is a result of the stuffing feelings down with which we feel unable to cope. It is equivalent to stuffing socks into a bag until it is bulging. The emotions are suppressed, cramped together, and ultimately become toxic to the body and soul. Despair, on the other hand, is experienced when we have the courage to feel the sadness appropriate to the loss of anything or anyone that we valued. It is the emptiness, the void… a void that cannot be filled until it is felt.

Feeling your despair is embracing it. It is standing in the center of the space once filled with your loved one and allowing yourself to confront the bareness of his or her absence. It is the last stage of letting go of the physical way you have related to the person. It is feeling the vacancy that has been left now that he or she is gone. Once you can endure that emptiness, and let go of the attachment to relating to your loved one in physical form only, the space can be filled with the new vibration of a transcended relationship.

It is becoming more and more evident that the only distance between the physical and non-physical worlds is the space we in the physical, hold on to by being so attached to what we knew. Once we let go, we can expand our awareness, and it is there, in a higher vibrational state, that we can connect with the essence of those we love. When a person dies, he or she does release the density of the physical plane. But the vibration of their soul–their essence lives on. Mediums and psychics around the world can confirm this with evidence that leaves little doubt. When you embrace that void in the physical, you clear the room for your own vibration to be elevated energetically to the point where you can once again feel the connection with your loved one.

I remember when my father died I described the feeling as his having moved to a new phone number and, for awhile, I did not know how to reach him. But when he did contact me I was ready to receive and respond. I have had access to a relationship with him ever since that time. The same experience has occurred with mom.

That is why I have said throughout this material that love does not die. That vortex of love that mom and I created in those last few months of her life is a state of expanded awareness I can access any time I want to feel close to her. It has also created a connection by which she can make contact with me–which, periodically, she does.

I do still have moments of sadness–of wishing she were in this dimension with me to share events in life in this realm. But those moments are not gut-wrenching. They are momentary. They do not distract from the connection I feel to her in my heart. So I encourage you to embrace this stage of your loss for it truly is the gateway to your eternal connection with those you love.

How do you do this? You simply breathe through it. Allow the void to be embraced. From this allowance comes the resurgence of something new. For this re-emergence to occur, you have to put a form to, and embrace, your despair. Use the focus questions below to assist you.

FOCUS QUESTIONS: To prepare for your EFT sequences respond to the following questions in your journal.

1. Take a moment to describe your life without the object of your love.

2. How is your life be different?

3. What do you miss the most about your loved one?

4. Recall one of your favorite, most loving, moments with your loved one. Describe this memory in as much detail as you can recall. Focusing on this memory recreates the vibration of love from which you will draw when you begin to allow the new form of relationship to emerge.

Suggested Exercise – Write a letter to your loved telling him or her all that you are going to miss about sharing your day-to-day life. Say what you were perhaps unable to say when they were still in physical form. Say what you may not even have known you felt when your loved one was still in physical form. Put it all down on paper.

When we write our feelings out like this, we get the energy of the feelings out of our body. We externalize the feelings thus bringing them from the unconscious to the conscious mind. The feelings are then more stimulated and present in the energetic meridian system and therefore more susceptible to being neutralized and released.

Each of the focus questions and journal exercises above will assist you in embracing your despair more fully. The more you allow that emptiness to be there the more room you will have to allow the relationship to morph into a new form.

When you feel the complete focus on all you have recorded. Keep this in mind as you tap on your karate point at least three times for each statement.

"Even though I felt/feel sad, despair, or hopeless in this situation (imagine it in your mind's eye) I love myself fully and completely."

Even though this sadness is almost more than I can bear, I realize it is a testament to my feelings for my loved one. The more I can let myself feel this sadness the more I will be able to embrace a new form of love with him or her.

So even though this hurts, I trust the process of my grief, and I want to fully embrace this release because I do truly love myself and my loved one enough to experience this loss.

Tap on the end points 5 to 6 times while you state your reminder phrases. Use the ones below but make up your own until you sense you have truly exhausted your despair and you are ready to move on.

Side of the eye: *This sadness.*

Corner of the eye: *This despair.*

Under the eye: *It feels so big, so endless.*

Upper lip: *How will I ever exist without my love?*

Lower lip: *God, this hurts.*

Collarbone: *I don't know how much more I can bear!*

Under the arm: *I feel so empty and alone.*

Chest bone: *Will I ever feel complete again?*

Head: *This emptiness and despair fill me up at my core.*

Side of the eye: *But maybe I can begin to let go... let go of this his sadness.*

Corner of the eye: *This despair.*

Under the eye: *It is big, but it's not endless. I am beginning to believe there is something beyond that will enable me to connect.*

Upper lip: *Maybe I can exist without my love?*

Lower lip: *God, even though this does hurt.*

Collarbone: *Maybe I can let go on and find a new form of our love.*

Under the arm: *A love where I don't feel so empty and alone.*

Chest bone: *Where I can feel complete again?*

Head: *Maybe in letting go I can find this new form of our love, one that penetrates this veil of separation, so I don't feel so alone.*

Continue tapping on the end points saying your reminder phrases until you experience a shift in your energy, and you truly feel ready to move on... until you really can entertain the idea that a new love can take form.

STAGE FIVE–RESOLUTION AND ACCEPTANCE–This stage is when you resolve the grief related to your current loss. You are ready to allow a new form of the relationship to unfold. You have embraced each stage of your loss, and have dealt with the void. You are now ready to replenish with something new–to replace the old form of your love with a new form, a form as of yet, unknown.

This final stage is when your adult self gets to make peace with the loss because you have dealt with the feelings of the immediate loss. The loss is replaced with a feeling of wholeness, of being complete. Trust in self, and your Higher Power are restored. The healing of the residual losses endured by your inner child will soon begin.

But first, you want to complete this process with your adult self. This completion comes when you sense you are ready to address the higher purpose of your loss. You are ready to go into meditation with your healing team and inquire about the purpose of your loss. You are receptive to asking how the resolution of your loss can benefit you spiritually and contribute to the expansion of your Soul.

When we address our healing in such a way, we move from being a victim of our loss to being a student of it. We recognize the spiritual significance of this loss. We begin to understand that embracing the stages of grief so courageously, and accepting our loss so authentically, opens our hearts. It expands our consciousness and enables us to see our life without our loved one differently. We come to understand more and more that there truly is no loss. We may have experienced signs or visitations–those extraordinary experiences that give us the inclination that our loved one has not gone far. We begin to comprehend that there is merely a change in the form of the relationship.

But this all begins when we are ready for the higher purpose of our pain to be revealed. The following exercise will help move you in this direction. However, this pursuit is one that will continue indefinitely. It has been twenty-two years since my father passed away, and I continue to learn from the relationship we have today. The evolution is truly endless.

EXERCISE: GUIDED MEDITATION ON "EXPLORING THE HIGHER PURPOSE OF YOUR LOSS."

PART ONE*: "God only gives us what we can handle."*

1. *Take a moment to picture the source of your loss in your mind's eye. Tune into the vibration of your heart. Notice how your heart was attached to that which you lost? How did you respond to the loss at the time of its occurrence? Ask who inside felt such grief and what does he or she need from you now? How do you want to respond to this pain and loss? Comfort your little one and assure him or her that you are going to assist in resolving the hurt, the sadness, the anger, and despair. But now is not the time. Now you need to step away from the depth of the loss and look at the loss through the eyes of your elevated self.*

You may want to return to the breathing exercises in which you bridged from your adult self to your higher self. It is from this expanded state of consciousness that you can begin to address questions of this higher, spiritual nature. When, as adults, we have an understanding of the higher purpose of our pain we are in a much better position to later assist our more fragile inner child in dealing with his or her original experience of the loss of safety and love.

PART TWO: *"I am willing to see the bigger picture of my Loss."*

1. *Now imagine you are standing before your guardians and your higher self. Ask about the higher purpose of this loss. What was it your Soul wanted you to experience in dealing with this loss? What was its purpose? What were its promise and reward?*

2. *Record your responses to this interaction with your healing team. Consider the following:*

    a. *What are your thoughts about this higher, more spiritual perspective on your recent loss?*

    b. *How are you now different than you were before enduring and resolving this loss?*

    c. *How have you grown?*

Now that you have an understanding of the higher purpose of your loss you are ready to use your tapping to anchor in that experience. This stage of your tapping is ultimately what energetically changes the vibration of your heart and soul. The following sequence will get you started.

Simply tap on your end points repeatedly as you recite the paragraph below. Keep tapping until you feel the "buzz."

Explanation of the "buss"… the buzz is usually felt as a tingling all over your body, or a surge of energy up your spine. According to quantum physicists, this surge signals that the neurons in your brain are firing the neurotransmitters that support the emotional response or vibrational response to this affirmation. According to the Teachings of Abraham, if you hold this "buzz" for 17 seconds it energetically takes the vibrational form needed for it to be launched as a desire. If you hold it for 68 seconds, your DNA begins to replicate the picture and attract its vibrational match. This is the straight law of attraction principle. Keep this in mind as you are redirecting your attention to a new form of connection with your loved one.

Tap as you read this...

I am now ready to fully let go and allow this new evolution to occur. I have honored my loved one and my relationship with him or her. I really am ready to expand my consciousness –to vibrationally merge with my higher self–for it is from that vibrational point I can connect with my loved one in the unseen. There truly is no separation between the physical and the nonphysical–it's just that in this vibration of energy my loved one cannot be seen. But I now truly understand it does not mean that he or she is not there. There does not have to be a void–a loss. The vibrational connection has merely changed. I can expand enough to connect in a new way. I now have the courage to do just that.

You may want to add variations to this meditative tapping sequence, but those words should give you the idea of what you are trying to accomplish. When you feel that connection is secure proceed to your last tapping sequence for processing the grief of your adult self which will prepare you to address the unresolved grief of your inner child. There may be other momentary flashes of anxiety, anger, or despair. But you have given yourself a model for breathing and tapping through those responses to your grief to the point where you will never be a victim to your loss again.

This last tapping sequence of this section is one you might find yourself using repeatedly. That's fine. Grief is organic. Customize the words to fit your needs, but know that as long as you are tapping, whatever you feel will diminish and become more manageable.

Even though there are still parts of me that do not want to let go, I can see the bigger picture. I am ready to embrace this current grief so I can be free to dig deeper into the grief of my wounded inner child.

"So even though I have been very courageous in dealing with the feelings of this current loss, I recognize I have an opportunity here to dig

a little deeper and begin to address the unresolved grief I experienced as a child.

So even though for decades I have held this belief and experience of not being safe–I am now open to the possibility of resolving all loss, realizing there truly is no reason to feel unsafe when I am connected to my higher self and the Divine.

Side of the eye: *I have shown myself that I can befriend this process of grief and am clear enough now to help my inner child heal.*

Corner of the eye: *I really appreciate my courage to feel the depth of my grief. I am now ready to assist the younger part of me so together we can heal.*

Under the eye: *I know there will be other levels to my grief, but I now trust my ability to cope.*

Upper lip: *I might feel more layers of sadness, despair, and even anger, but I truly have the confidence I can now cope.*

Lower lip: *I'm no longer afraid to feel.*

Collarbone: *I understand my loved one is just on the other side, a different vibration that can still be felt.*

Under the arm: *We merely differ in our vibrational frequency. But if I am willing to relate, my loved one will respond.*

Chest bone: *I've had the courage to face my fears, my anger, and despair, and the reward is this continued love.*

Head: *There is no loss. I am now ready to embrace that truth, and this gives me the courage to help my younger ones heal.*

Moving from the Possibility of Change to Conviction–When ready continue with the next phase of your tapping as you move into the possibility of letting go and moving on.

Side of the eye: *Love doesn't die.*

Corner of the eye: *There is no death.*

Under the eye: *There is a change in the vibration which I now understand.*

Upper lip: *I have the courage to love.*

Lower lip: *I feel full of life.*
Collarbone: *There is nothing I have to fear.*
Under the arm: *I embrace this experience…*
Chest bone: *I am willing to share this experience…*
Head:… *with others as well as with my inner child.*

You have freed up the energy you had tied up in your grief. You can now work with the residue of your past; learn about your inner child's pain, bring him or her home. You can now assure those parts of you that they can be free to feel their feelings. You will not abandon them in their pain. You will get the help you need, pray for the guidance required, so you can assist them in letting go and feeling safe. Your current loss inspired this healing so you can now truly live your life without fear.

Healing Your Inner Child's Grief

EXPLORING THE FIVE STAGES OF GRIEF FOR THE INNER CHILD

Inevitably, when we suffer a loss as an adult, the residue of the past comes to haunt us. I remember what occurred when, as an adult, I lost my first pet. A plethora of unresolved grief erupted. It felt as though I were crying every tear I had ever repressed. The floodgates opened. The depth of feeling overwhelmed and frightened me. Luckily I had a talented counselor who helped me navigate through the rocky terrain of my unresolved childhood losses thath ad been triggered.

In my case, not only did my childhood grief emerge. The multi-dimensional grief of the history of my soul seemed to collide with events in my present life. I found myself engulfed in a grief for which I had no context. The tools and methods I offer in this material apply to processing grief from other dimensions and times. At some points, you will even see reference to this occurrence. But the book that explores a multidimensional bleed–through, as I call it, and gives you the methods to heal on that level, is my book called, "Which Lifetime Is This Anyway?" It is available through my website, or you can purchase it from Amazon.com.

For the sake of "Beyond Compassion," I will be focusing primarily on exercises borrowed from my signature 7-Layer Healing Process that first introduced energy tapping as a viable method to address the wounds of your fragile selves. Not only will you find it useful for healing your inner child's grief–it addresses building the relationship between you and the adult and that wounded within which empowers you to resolve a myriad of unresolved feelings from childhood whether they are related to an actual concrete loss or not. As you will see each of us has that point in our childhood where we first experienced the world as unsafe. The intensity of that loss may differ, but loss affects all of us nonetheless.

So we will begin where it all begins. We begin with the first time our ability to cope was threatened. Whether remembered or not, there was that moment in your life when you first felt loss. The circumstances may not be the same as another, but the impact was the same; you froze. That moment in time is called the essential wound.

THE ESSENTIAL WOUND

Each of us experiences a defining moment in our lives when we realize we are not safe. It is our first moment of loss. It is part of the human experience. Hal Bennett, in his book, _Follow Your Bliss,_ referred to this moment as the "essential wound." Our psyche experiences the loss of safety which shatters our basic assumption about our world. Things in our life begin to go awry. What we thought would lead to safety all of a sudden does not. This loss of safety can result from neglect, sexual or physical abuse, or mental cruelty through shame and belittlement. It can be experienced in this lifetime or can even be carried over from a previous lifetime. Quantum physics suggests that the DNA blueprint of our first remembered soul experience of being unsafe can be transmitted through the etheric body to our physical body and impact the force field of our current incarnation.

In response to this realization, we experience that first stage of grief. Irrespective of its origin, our psyche goes into shock. We either dissociate from the emotion of the event or bury recall of the event, thus banishing the memory deep into the unconscious mind. The stress of these traumas, however, gets recorded in the electrical systems of our bodies and ultimately emerges as symptoms of what is called Post Traumatic Stress Disorder. There are two kinds of PTSD: simple and complex. Complex PTSD usually results from multiple incidents of abuse and violence such as child abuse or domestic violence. Simple PTSD is related to an isolated incident which is beyond the scope of ordinary coping abilities, such as 911 or a natural disaster.

Post Traumatic Stress Disorder-PTSD

Until recently it was thought that PTSD impacted only combat veterans or victims of isolated, one-time events such as 911. Now scientists know that, in fact, another form of PTSD, called complex PTSD, exists. Survivors of atrocities such as the Holocaust, torture, war, natural disasters, catastrophic illnesses, and horrific accidents are obviously susceptible to PTSD. But research shows that in fact, anyone who is exposed to an on-going threat to his or her safety, such as physical or sexual abuse, rape, domestic violence, family alcoholism, or any experience which threatens one's basic survival, can develop a form of PTSD.

Remarkably, this holds true even if a person *witnesses* a traumatic event. If, as a child, you observed the abuse of your mother or the abuse of a sibling, you can develop debilitating PTS symptoms from just having been a witness. Traumas of great magnitude shatter our basic assumption about the world and our personal safety. The impact can leave us feeling alienated, distrustful, or overly clinging. These responses are buried and emerge only when there is a trigger which brings these feelings back to the surface.

Loss in adulthood serves as this trigger. Underneath the surface, the electrically-charged emotions related to these losses are forever coded in our bodies and are conditioning our cells to attract exactly that which we most fear. The process becomes circular—our fear perpetuates this Post Traumatic Stress response, and our PTS response perpetuates our fear. Fear creates anxiety. Anxiety is the first stage of grief. We are perpetually responding to the never-ending loss of our true self. Why? Because when we feel unsafe, we deny our true self and develop the adapted self as we evolve into the person we think we need to be to be loved and protected.

THE BIO-CHEMICAL PERSPECTIVE

Author, Candace Pert—a neuroscientist who is also featured in the film *"What the Bleep Do We know?"* provides a very compelling, biochemical explanation for the circular impact of our perpetual grief. When asked why we keep getting into the same kinds of relationships, having the same kinds of arguments, repeating the same patterns, she replies,

"…Every emotion circulates through our body as chemicals called neuropeptides—"short-chain" amino acids—that talk to every cell of our body deciding what is worth paying attention to. When these peptides repeatedly bombard the receptor sites, the sites become less sensitive and require more peptides to be stimulated. Receptors actually begin to crave the neuro-peptides they are designed to receive. In this sense, our bodies become addicted to emotional states. When we have repeated experiences that generate the same emotional response, our bodies develop an appetite for these experiences. Like addicts, we will draw experiences toward us that give us that fix…"

When constantly exposed to neglect and abuse, we develop an almost hyper-vigilant anticipation of the abuse—and when we anticipate it, we attract and create it.

Lynn Grabhorn, in her best-selling book entitled, " Excuse Me, Your Life Is Waiting," states *"Modern-day physicists have finally come to agree that energy and matter are one and the same… everything vibrates because of everything—what you can see and not see—is energy, pure, pulsing, ever-flowing energy. Just like the sound which pours out of a musical instrument, some energy vibrates fast from high frequencies, and some vibrate slowly at low frequencies. The energy that flows out from us comes from our highly-charged emotions which create highly charged electromagnetic wave patterns of energy, making us powerful—but volatile—walking magnets. "Like attracts like." When we're experiencing anything that isn't joy or love, such as fear, worry, guilt… we are sending out low-frequency vibrations… they're going to attract only cruddy stuff back to us… It is always a vibrational match."*

In my over three decades of experience helping individuals arrest their addictive behavior and heal their childhood and soul wounds, I have observed this same dynamic from a slightly different angle. I have observed that most of us when conditioned to anticipate a certain response, attempt to manage the anxiety and fear which accompany that anticipation. Our psyches cannot sustain the on-going experience of anxiety which ultimately develops into the symptoms of our PTSD. In an attempt to manage our emotions we flip between the second, third, and fourth, stages of grief which are bargaining, rage, and despair.

CO-DEPENDENT BARGAIN VERSUS SELF-PRESERVING RAGE AND DESPAIR

When individuals muster up enough courage to begin the process of confronting their childhood pain, it becomes apparent that at a very young age they often faced an experience which shattered their basic sense of safety. In response, they either became active in early co-dependent behavior; lashed out in anger at others, or shut down, became sullen, depressed, and closed off to feeling anything. I call this the *fight, flight or make it right* response! If we are caught in the pattern of trying to fix things around us, make things right, or keep everything under control, our underlying anxiety results in an emotional freeze.

Our "co-dependent" behavior masks this freeze and temporarily wards off the tension of the unknown. We try to keep all of our ducks in a row to stay safe. All responses are attempts to cover up the underlying feeling of loss related to believing we are not good enough to be loved and protected. We begin to believe the problem is with us.

Our parents are not protecting us or making us feel safe because there is something wrong with us. Sometimes they even said this was the case. This belief of unworthiness becomes the source of our negative self-talk, and it sets off the cycle of the shame/blame game.

THE CYCLE OF SHAME AND BLAME

Our shame is the source of our self-incriminations. We assume we need to be perfect to be loved. When we fail, we feel shame, or we project the shameful feelings onto others and blame them for our deficiencies and disappointments. We super-impose the experiences of our past onto the situations of our present. The faces of strangers become the faces of those who betrayed and disappointed us. We forever get caught in the cycle of feeling shame for not being good enough or placing blame on anyone who disappoints, threatens, or hurts, us. The shame/blame game creates a cycle which is never-ending, and that cycle is this process of grief.

We have worked with these five stages in response to a current, adult, loss. But let's now look at this residual grief–grief that we are too young to process–through the lens of the child within us. Again, the process of grief has five stages. The first stage is panic and is experienced in the form of our PTSD. To manage this panic, we fluctuate between the second, third, and fourth, stages of grief. We bargain, rage, or feel despair.

If we get caught in the loop of the second stage, we bargain with the experience by attempting to make deals with the lost object in hopes of retrieving it. If the loss is our sense of safety, we attempt to retrieve that safety by fixing the situation which resulted in the loss in the first place. If a loss such as this occurs in childhood, we develop behaviors whose intent is to win back the favor of the disapproving or abusive parent. Our bargain goes something like this…*"Mommy, if I am a good little girl and never make you angry—then will you love me enough to make me feel safe?"* Of course, we can never be perfect enough to be re-instated to this sense of safety. We can perpetually get caught in the bargaining stage of grief enacted through our co-dependent behavior of trying. We can spend lifetimes trying to be re-instated!

When this does not work, we shift between the third and fourth stages of grief—anger, and despair. If your anger is turned outward and projected onto others, you are operating in the third stage of grief. If the anger is turned inward in the form of depression or despair, you are operating in the fourth stage of grief. Until your grief is processed through expression and neutralized with a technique such as EFT, you will be forever caught in the vicious cycle.

Our PTSD activates our need to manage this discomfort. We react by either a fight (anger), flight (despair) or make it right (co-dependency) response. We may find moments of peace—but the cycle of our grief is raging just below the surface and emerges whenever we encounter a situation which resonates with our original, essential, wound.

THE SHAME OF OUR IMPERFECTIONS

The motivating force behind the grief process—and its perpetual re-enactment—is our feeble attempt to ward off the insurmountable fear of abandonment and loss resulting from the shame of our imperfections. The panic which accompanies this ever-present fear is intolerable. It fuels the inner child's sabotage. It continually circulates through our body sending messages to our cells that not only are we not safe (which triggers panic), but our lack of safety is our fault (which triggers shame). We come to believe we are not worthy and lovable enough to be protected. We unconsciously hold onto the hope that if we can just be good enough—perfect enough—"they" will come through for us and be able and willing to love us and make us feel safe. This inner belief becomes the foundation of our need to be perfect. Our pursuit of perfection gives us a focus for the tension created by the fear we may fail.

But we do fail. We fail because there is no such thing as perfection. When we fail, we end up back in the middle of the tumultuous emotions of our essential wound—the fear—the panic—the disconnection from our true self. We end up back in the cycle of grief.

This cycle is the essence of the twists and bends in our DNA make-up. It is the root of our energy disturbances and energetic imbalances.

It is this biochemical response which reinforces this pattern over and over and keeps continually bombarding the receptor sites with the peptides which disarm us.

LET THE HEALING BEGIN

To become fulfilled and healthy adults who can manifest our heart's desire we have to intervene in this cycle. We have to revise our *false belief* that we are not good enough and challenge our *pursuit of perfection.* We have to grieve the original loss of safety—express and process the anger and despair of the Post Traumatic Stress associated with our loss, and ultimately reprogram the cellular encoding of our DNA. Combining the breathing exercises with *Interactive Tapping*™ sequences to addresses this.

REVISING YOUR FALSE BELIEF—CHALLENGING YOUR PURSUIT OF PERFECTION

This formula begins by dealing with the mental body and the belief systems which developed in response to your inner child not feeling safe. The mental body or mind carries the need to understand. It is the part of you who reads with such diligence to try to make sense of what happened and what needs to happen for things to change.

Knowledge is power. When you come to know that the only true source of safety is the Divine, you step into your empowerment and can orchestrate your own healing.

As John Bradshaw stated in the mid-eighties, "There is no human security!"

The only way to challenge the belief system of your perfectionism—the source of your shame—the belief that you are not good enough—is to operate from the illuminated, adult self. It is he or she who is connected enough to the Higher Source to be able to respond to, and retrieve, the wounded inner child or soul part who felt the loss in the first place. That wounded self will let go of the old belief system when he or she experiences a different reality in the interaction with this illuminated you. You are the one your inner child awaits. You create your reality, and therefore, are empowered to envision a new experience for this wounded self.

You begin with the breathing exercises I introduced earlier. In your mind's eye, you breathe and tap on your chakras as you reconnect to your Higher Self. Each breath you take inflates you with the essence of the Divine. You begin your life with your first breath, and your life ends with your last breath. Each breath-from birth to death-gives you the opportunity to reconnect. Once connected, you can retrieve the adapted self; neutralize his or her feelings with my *Interactive Tapping*™ formula and create whatever reality he or she needs to feel safe. Remember, *the mind does not know the difference between what is real or imagined. What you can conceive, you can achieve. What you do not resist-you allow.*

GRIEVING THE ORIGINAL LOSS WITH INTERACTIVE TAPPING™

Targeting your inner child's grief with *Interactive Tapping*™ *sequences* offers a viable method for your adult self to neutralize the effects of your childhood anxiety and grief. When this anxiety is neutralized, the inner child witnesses that he or she can survive.

In fact, being rescued by the adult self is proof of this. You now have a part of you who can escort the wounded self through all of the feelings of grief and the interactive tapping™ sequences provide the vehicle to succeed. You can step into your empowered self with your breathing, and then use energy tapping to support your vulnerable self through the panic as you neutralize the franticness of trying to control the situation.

By neutralizing this frantic need to bargain, you can move into the rage of the loss. The adult self helps the inner child get the anger out of his or her body. And when the inner child has expressed and neutralized the rage he or she can collapse into despair. True despair is standing in the center of the void of the loss. It is developing the ability to tolerate the emptiness. Your inner child has no need to distract with your addictions. He or she does not have to deny with disruptions.

You stand side by side with your inner child naked in the truth of the loss of safety, and embrace its rawness without fear, because the inner child trusts that safety can now be restored.

The tumultuous emotions of your essential wound emerge to be neutralized, so the emotions resulting from your PTSD can subside. They have found release and give way to a calm which can only be experienced once the truth has been spoken. This experience is true whether you are dealing with the memory of an inner child or the recall of an aspect of your soul. When you have successfully reconnected with your authentic self and neutralized and released the emotions, the circuitry of both the physical and etheric bodies is forever changed. As an empowered adult you can download a new program into the DNA make-up of each cell. This task is accomplished through the interaction which occurs when you use tapping as a method to relate to, and heal, your inner child.

REPROGRAMMING YOUR DNA WITH SOURCE ENERGY AND INTERACTIVE TAPPING SEQUENCES

First of all, DNA is a large molecule, shaped like a double helix, and found primarily in the chromosomes of the cell nucleus. The DNA contains the genetic information of the cell. The DNA forms a double helix, two elongated molecular chains (like staircases) that wrap around each other. DNA tells our cells what they have been; what they will continue to be; and what they will become. The DNA is the blueprint for our life processes. Each cell of our body contains the complete genetic code for the whole body.

According to Margaret Ruby, founder of *The Possibilities DNA Vibrational Healing School,* "*...Our body's communication systems have been broken down due to feelings from limiting beliefs. There is a vibrational interference pattern attached to this limiting belief causing negative, low vibrational emotions, which affect and distort our DNA. When two energy waves (thoughts and feelings) pass the same point and are out of phase, they interact and create a low vibrational, low wave interference that can, in turn, create a physical or emotional imbalance.*

Our DNA then replicates this interference pattern which has a twist and slight bend to it…"

**These twists and bends have to be neutralized if we are to heal
And manifest a productive, successful, and satisfactory life.**

Dr. Joe Dispenza—also featured in *"What the Bleep Do We know?"* comments, *"…the remarkable component to this dynamic is the fact that as our cells split—and they do split and recreate—they carry the energy of the old cell. It does not split with a fresh start. A cell's off-spring carries the imprint of the parent cell at the time of the split. Negativity begets negativity, and positive reinforcement begets positive reinforcement!"*

There are trillions of cells in your body. Within each and every cell there is the nucleus, the mastermind for the blueprint of your life. The stories recorded in your DNA determine the course of your relationships, your wealth, your health, and your career. What happens to you on your life journey is a result of what is written in the life code of your DNA. When this blueprint becomes faulty—the communication between each cell is faulty. This faulty communication is in response to the wounds experienced in childhood. It is established in response to the fears, disappointments, and hurts, encountered when you were unable to fend for yourself.

Connecting with your Higher Self by using the breathing exercises you were introduced to in the last section enables the adult self to repair this faulty communication. By activating your DNA and reprogramming it with the vibration of the divine or spiritual energy your most illuminated self re-establishes a connection with its intuition. The wounded inner child can then do the same. The twists and bends, which create the interference patterns of the DNA in every cell in your body, are neutralized, and the cells can once again be infused with this vibration of Divine Energy. The *Interactive Tapping*™ Sequences offered at each respective stage of this process effectively alters the DNA messages of your cells and empowers you to successfully attract that which you want and deserve.

WEBSITE RESOURCES FOR THIS SECTION

Dr. Masaru Emoto—http://www.masaru-emoto.net/

Dr. Candace Pert—http://www.candacepert.com/

Hal Bennett—http://www.halzinabennett.com/

Lynn Grabhorn—http://www.lynngrabhorn.net/

Margaret Ruby—http://www.possibilitiesdna.com/home.html

Dr. Joe Dispenza—http://www.drjoedispenza.com/

What The Bleep Do We Know? http://www.whatthebleep.com/

Post Traumatic Stress Disorder—http://www.headinjury.com/faqptsd.htm

DNA Graphic—http://www.ucsc.edu/currents/00-01/07-03/haussler.html

How our Past and Present Collide

Again, your essential wound occurred at the precise moment you realized you were not safe. You went into a panic and experience terror you would not survive. This moment is the origin of your Post Traumatic Stress Disorder.

It is this underlying trauma that gets reactivated whenever we experience a major loss such as that I described in this story. Symptoms of our PTS get activated anytime we experience a situation in our day-to-day life that resonates at all with the original neglect, judgment, shame, or abuse. The unresolved feelings related to this first experience of loss determine how we navigate through the feelings of the current losses irrespective of their intensity.

As I stated in the general overview of grief, all feelings encountered as a human being can be linked in some way to the five stages of grief. Therefore, in helping your inner child process the unresolved emotions of childhood, whether they are labeled as grief or not, build the relationship with him or her that restores the trust. This restoration is necessary for dealing with the present-day loss because the intensity of your loss as an adult is fueled by the unresolved emotions you experienced as a child.

In the previous section, you dealt with the immediate feelings of loss–those related directly to the recent loss. In this next section, you begin to dig deeper into those unresolved issues from your past–those issues which fuel your current response to life in ways you can now begin to recognize and resolve.

SO LET'S BEGIN TO WORK WITH THESE STAGES OF GRIEF WHICH WE EACH FACE AS WE ENCOUNTER OUR LIFE'S CHALLENGES AND TRIUMPHS.

A Note on Tapping for the Inner Child: The tapping process I will be facilitating for each stage of your inner child's grief uses the same three setup phrases to identify the unresolved feelings that would inhibit your inner child's ability to grieve. Creating an affirmation for the acceptance of the way in which your inner child coped is one of the first steps in winning the trust of your inner child. It is acknowledging the inner child's response to his or her situation while neutralizing any judgment you, as the adult, might have about the manner in which you, as a child, coped. This acceptance establishes the platform to begin to heal.

The sequences are then again divided into two, progressive sections. You first neutralize the negative thoughts and feelings your inner child had at the time of the loss. Sometimes you are speaking to the inner child and sometimes, when using the pronoun, "I, you are giving your inner child a voice. I suggest you stay with each series of the sequences until you feel an energetic shift that signifies your inner child is ready to move to the next round. However, be patient. Often this is the first time your inner child has been able to speak his or her true feelings about the trauma and fear experienced in childhood.

Also, though it is important to give your little one the room to vent, it is equally important to do so while you are tapping. Remember, tapping sends the electrical impulse through your body to untie the knot of tension experienced when you target these unresolved feelings.

It is the tapping itself that ensures the feelings are being neutralized. To vent with no recourse for dissolution can lead to your ruminating and feeling retriggered all over again with no reprieve or resolve.

The second set of sequences introduces the possibility of change. This shift in the focus of the tapping softens the psyche and invites your inner child to consider the possibility that it is safe to trust the inner adult. This is a new concept for your inner child. He or she is not used to feeling accepted and allowed to speak. The last statements of tapping should leave you feeling strong and energized. They should reflect the shift in your inner child from fear to trust. Use the statements I have provided as an example but definitely customize your own sequences as well. Only you know exactly what needs to be targeted with respect to your childhood experience. Once this shift is accomplished, the two of you will be ready to progressively proceed through each of the respective stages of grief.

Keep in mind what the inner child is grieving is the original loss of safety. If there were an actual loss, such as the death of a parent, or the trauma of a divorce, these situations would need to be targeted more specifically. But for now, you are just working with the residue of the loss of safety that may have gotten triggered by your recent loss. For a deeper healing that is more age-specific, I recommend you obtain a copy of "*The Inner Child Workbook.*" Each developmental stage includes a section with instructions on how to help that particular inner child grieve. It can most easily be purchased through amazon. com.

STAGE ONE–DENIAL, PANIC AND ANXIETY–THE INITIAL AND CURRENT RESPONSE TO THE LOSS

To reiterate, because we were too young to endure the panic and survive, we went into shock and experienced a numbing denial of the truth. Our body stored this pain in our electrical circuitry, and we developed what is called *Chronic Post Traumatic Stress Disorder.* Some of us dissociated and went into that dark hole previously referenced. Our emotional system simply shut down.

If, as an adult, you experience a lack of affect, or it seems as though emotional expressiveness is a missing, it is a sign that your inner child split off because he or she could not endure the pain. Sandra Ingerman's book, *"Soul Retrieval,"* refers to this as "Soul Loss." Her book covers this subject in much more detail than I am prepared to address in this material, but *"Soul Retrieval"* is certainly a worthwhile read and can also be purchased through amazon.com.

These next two exercises will assist you in identifying the possible soul loss your inner child experienced that is now resurfacing in response to your current loss.

Exercise 1–*Ponder your current loss. When you bring focus to the feelings, you are now experiencing try to recall the first remembered experience when you felt a similar set of emotions. Follow the thread of your emotions. Let that tension escort you back to that first remembered experience. Don't force it, just trust whatever thoughts or images emerge. This will give you an idea of the essential wound that may have been triggered. Then record your thoughts in your journal.*

Exercise 2–*Now take this experience one step further. When you experienced or re-experienced, this loss, and you did, or perhaps do not, have the mechanisms to cope, the energy is diverted. Think for a moment how you may have diverted your attention from this set of feelings related to your current loss. Usually we react with some excessive behavior.*

In fact, it is most likely from this arena your addictive behaviors emerged. So, think for a moment, how you cut off from the feelings with which you could not cope. Did you ignore them? Did you compulsively or addictively act out? Take a moment to make a list of the ways you acted out (and perhaps still do) to keep yourself from feeling the panic or discomfort of your loss. In other words, write down ways you have kept or keep yourself in denial!

Record any thoughts you might have on this list in your journal.

Exercise 3-Take a plain piece of paper and draw a great big garbage bag in the center of the page. It can be something as simple as this…

Now write in the center of that garbage bag all the thoughts, feelings, and events, associated with your anxiety, denial, and panic. Include everything from your perspective, as well as from your inner child's perspective, that you want to tap on and ultimately release.

Once done have this garbage bag sitting in front of you. As you tap, know that your psyche is neutralizing everything you have put in that bag. The procedure is called, "bundling the baggage." It was developed by EFT Master Lindsay Kinney and is very effective in the processing of feelings associated with one subject. Everything that is written down and symbolically placed in the bag is neutralized by your psyche as you tap on the respective points of release.

EFT FOR ANXIETY

Now combine these feelings and thoughts you have just dislodged with your tapping. While continuously tapping on your karate end point state each of the following setup statements at least three times:

Even though I felt anxious in this situation-and I know I have felt this anxiety before-I can feel it in the pit of my stomach, the back of my neck, or in the stress, I hold in my shoulders, I love myself fully and completely.

Even though I feel great anxiety in response to this loss, I now choose to work with this fear, release it from my body, so I can begin to resolve this residual grief of my inner child.

Even though I am experiencing great anxiety about this situation, I choose to believe I am in the arms of my Higher Power and, with that support, I choose, as the adult self, to begin to help my inner child express and release his or her fear.

Neutralizing the Negative for your inner child…

Side of the eye: *Really feel anxious… feel it in my stomach, shoulders, or neck.*

Corner of the eye: *He/she believes the loss cannot be survived…*

Under the eye: *Really frightened regarding this loss…*

Upper lip: *Afraid he or she won't survive…*

(Now switch to the voice of the inner child…)

Lower lip: *What if "I" don't survive…*

Collar bone: *So frightened I won't survive…*

Under the arm: *Just want this fear to go away…*

Chest bone: *So afraid I won't survive…*

Rib: *I'm too young to feel this afraid.*

Wrist: *Will it ever go away?*

Head: *This anxiety has been with me for so long…*

Moving from the Possibility of Change to Conviction…

Side of the eye: *Maybe if I bury myself in the arms of my Adult self…*

Corner of the eye: *Maybe I can let go and feel safe…*

Under the eye: *Please help me fill this emptiness…*

Upper lip: *Help me move beyond this gut-wrenching loss and fear…*

Lower lip: *Just want to feel safe…*

Collarbone: *Maybe with help, I can survive…*

Rib: *Maybe I can find the support to feel safe.*

Wrist: *I want to connect with my adult self and then let this fear go.*

Under the arm: *I want to trust…*

Chest bone: *I want to trust my adult self…*

Head: *He or she is trustworthy enough to help me survive.*

Keep tapping until you really feel the energetic shift of releasing and letting go. Customize your own reminder phrases so you can address the unique way he or she may experience this stage of grief.

Stage Two–Bargaining–*Making deals to manage the loss which was mitigated by your co-dependent bargain.*

Again, the co-dependent bargain is the contract we made as a child with a parental figure, or with God, in which we agreed to do something in hopes of being lovable enough to warrant their willingness to keep us safe. The problem is that the other party was either unaware of this agreement or unable or unwilling to live up to this agreement. Consequently, we ended up feeling betrayed and full of rage when confronted with the fact that our bargain was not kept.

As adults, we integrate the shame of this failure into our self–talk, and it becomes the basis of our internal critic and our projected, judgmental self. The culprit who perpetuates this self-talk and protects us with mal-adaptive coping mechanisms is what I referred to in the overview, as our *cherished saboteur.*

Exercise 1–*Let's now work with that bargain. This is directed to the parent to whom you are hoping will protect–the parent with whom you are compromising and bargaining in hopes of winning the approval needed to feel safe. Fill in the blanks according to what feels right.*

Example–*Mommy, I will be a good little girl, and do everything you ask, if only you will love me enough to stop hitting me so I can feel safe.*

Your Co-dependent Bargain _________, (*the parent with whom you are making the bargain*) I will_____________ (*the agreement you tried to make–i.e.e, "I will be perfect; I will be good"*) if only you will (*what we hoped to get in return*) "*keep me safe, you will love and protect me.*"

WRITE YOUR CO-DEPENDENT BARGAIN OUT:

Now bundle the baggage of all of your attempts to manage the situation over which you had no control… write in the center of that garbage bag all the thoughts, feelings, and events, associated with your attempts to bargain with your loss of safety as a child, the ways in which you compromised yourself in hopes of returning to a state of safety and peace. Include everything you can recall from your inner child's perspective, that you want to tap on and ultimately release.

EFT For Bargaining Stage

Tap on your karate point while stating the phrases below. Customize these to fit your needs.

Even though I tried but failed to control, fix, or change, this situation (imagine it in your mind's eye), I love myself fully and completely.

Even though I tried very hard to change this situation I was just a little kid. But it is so nice to feel that my adult self loves me anyway. There really wasn't anything I could do.

So even though I did try so very, very hard, I now realize it was not my place to alter this situation. I was too young. It is so comforting to now know that my adult self loves me enough to detach and accept the outcome for what it was. (PLEASE NOTE: If as the adult this does not resonate, return to the tapping sequences to clear yourself of the distraction and unwillingness to be present for the healing of your inner child. If you are still carrying judgment about how you as a child handled this situation then this needs to be neutralized with your tapping before you can be an effective agent of change for this fragile one within you.)

Next, use the following samples to begin your neutralization process. Add your own phrases accordingly, but continue to tap around the end points saying your reminder phrase until you have neutralized the negative, introduced the possibility of change, and feel conviction with respect to your new stance.

Neutralizing the Negative

Side of the eye: *Really tried so very hard…*

Corner of the eye: *Am exhausted with my attempts…*

Under the eye: *Just want to let it go…*

Upper lip: *But fight this need to control and fix…*

Lower lip: *It is so in my nature to jump in…*

Collarbone: *Wish I could just let go…*

Under the arm: *But this need to do something took over…*

Chest bone: *And I just didn't seem to be able to let it go…*

Rib: *Felt too much anxiety to let go…*

Wrist: *Hard to give up the hope…*

Head: *Wish I could have relaxed and let it go…*

Moving from the Possibility of Change to Conviction…

Side of the eye: *Maybe I can now begin to try something new…*

Corner of the eye: *Maybe I can turn to my adult self instead of feeling so scared…*

Under the eye: *Maybe what I can change is the way I respond…*

Upper lip: *Maybe I don't always have to be the one…*

Lower lip: *Maybe my adult self can be in charge…*

Collarbone: *Maybe my adult self can help me move through the need to respond…*

Under the arm: *I can give up control…*

Chest bone: *I can tolerate this panic and let it go…*

Rib: *I can let my adult self show me a new way of coping…*

Wrist: *I really want to respond in a new way…*

Head: *I feel strong and secure in my ability to trust and to let go!*

Keep tapping until you really feel the energetic shift of releasing and letting go. Customize your own reminder phrases so you can address the unique way you may experience this stage of grief.

Exercise 2–Designing a nurturing statement. *To heal this bargain your adult self needs to design a nurturing statement that counters the compromise–a loving statement this compromising, wounded one needs to hear in order to give up the bargain. Design that statement now.*

An example of adult self speaking to inner child – *"Honey, you do not have to do anything other than be yourself. I love you and promise not to ever hurt you. You are safe with me, and deserve all the love and protection I can, and am willing, giving."*

Now come up with your own statement that fits your unique co-dependent bargain. Record it in your journal.

Once you have your statement tap on the end points as you imagine saying this statement to your inner child. Keep saying it over and over until you feel a connection has been made. Let the healing of these words really sink into the inner child's awareness. State it slowly and with heart. You are anchoring this new belief system into the inner child's experience. The tapping neutralizes your inner child's doubt and fear while progressively reinforcing his or her willingness to believe and trust.

Exercise 3–*This exercise overrides the old belief system housed in the codependent bargain and replaces it with a new way of thinking based on the trust that has been restored to you and your inner child. In essence, this proclamation is what the adult self can now say to the inner child that is believable once this bargain has been dissolved and trust has been restored.*

Read each proclamation separately while repeatedly tapping on the end points. Read it first from the adult self to your inner child, and then, as your inner child, to your adult self. Customize the words if it feels right to do so.

PROCLAMATION FOR THE ADULT SELF–

I, ________, (state your name) AM WORTHY OF YOUR TRUST. YOU ARE A CHILD OF THE UNIVERSE AND DESERVE TO BE PROTECTED AT ALL TIMES. IT IS MY JOB AND MY HONOR TO LOVE YOU AND TO KEEP YOU SAFE._AND I PROMISE THAT IF I AM NOT PERFECT, AND IF THERE ARE MOMENTS WHEN I FLOUNDER AND DO NOT FOLLOW

THROUGH, I WILL HOLD MYSELF ACCOUNTABLE. I WILL ASSURE YOU IT WAS NOT YOUR FAULT, AND TOGETHER, WE WILL COME BACK INTO THE LIGHT WHERE WE CAN HEAL._

PROCLAMATION FOR THE INNER CHILD-

I, _________, (state your name) AM WORTHY OF YOUR LOVE. I AM A TRUE CHILD OF THE UNIVERSE. I CAN TRUST YOU, MY ADULT SELF. I NOW BELIEVE I DESERVE TO BE PROTECTED AT ALL TIMES, AND I TRUST THAT YOU WILL KEEP ME SAFE. I UNDERSTAND THERE MAY BE TIMES WHEN THIS IS NOT THE CASE, BUT I BELIEVE YOU WHEN YOU SAY THAT YOU WILL NOT ABANDON ME. YOUWILL NOT BLAME ME. INSTEAD, YOU WILL ACKNOWLEDGE YOUR MISTAKE AND TELL ME YOU ARE SORRY SO THAT TOGETHER WE CAN HEAL AND TRUST.

It is this kind of dialogue you and your inner child need to have to enable the two of you to deal with the more intimidating feelings of anger and rage.

STAGE THREE-ANGER-THE UNSPOKEN TRUTH.

Anger seeped into our inner child's experience when the denial and bargaining no longer worked. It was anger at the loss, agitation at the loss. But for most that anger could not be expressed. It had to be camouflaged or repressed and ultimately became the source of our negative self-image. As you read in the overview of the development of the inner child's pain, it is easier to collapse into shame and believe there is something wrong with us then to hold the anger at our parents for not being strong enough to love us in the way we deserved. Making it our fault gives us the false impression that there is something we can do to impact a situation about which we feel totally helpless.

If we were not muted and silenced then the anger was most likely discharged through more overt behaviors such as hyper-activity, or the development of Attention Deficient Disorders. Those behaviors let off steam, but the underlying feelings are never addressed. Few children are ever truly able to embrace the full essence of their anger.

Instead, we grew up with our truth remaining unspoken. The truth was that we did suffer a loss. And if we are ever to feel safe again that little part of us needs to acknowledge the truth of that loss, the gut-wrenching truth that he or she did not feel safe or protected.

Much of the anger you experience in your inner work is anger fueled by memories of loss experienced before you had the knowledge and tools to cope with it. The emotion was an instinctive response to feeling unsafe. What went unexpressed got lodged in the tissues of your body. And it remains there as an energy block (or, as Gary Craig, founder of EFT calls it, an energetic disturbance) until it can be physically released.

The thought of releasing anger is frightening for most people. The fear is that the anger will be endless. The fear is that if we take the cap off of our latent anger, we will not cope. But anger can be released, and it can be released in a constructive and beneficial way. To ensure this occurs I always recommend you begin your anger work with this simple exercise.

EXERCISE–Creating Protection – *To create the safety you and your inner child deserve begin by closing your eyes and imagining that you are surrounded by a bubble light. Set the intention with the universe that your anger be encased in this light. Ask that as you express the anger it be transmuted with a violet light. And finally, request that the energy of your anger be sent directly into the Great Central Sun to be transformed. This practice will seal your anger so that its energy does not bleed out into other arenas.*

When we truly trace the threads of our anger most often we discover that the anger comes back to our being angry at ourselves for not saying no, or for regrets about which we now feel shame. This anger is toxic–to us, and to all those around us.

But we soon come to understand that the unresolved anger emerging is the residue from the grief of the past. The child within us did not have the option to deal with the emotions in any other way. We begin to realize that it is this level of unrest from the unexpressed anger of our inner child that keeps us from resolving our grief and moving into another form of a relationship with our loved or the situation which was recently altered or lost. The residual anger has first to be identified before it can be released and resolved.

The first step to flushing out his or her anger is to weed out all of the negating statements that block this anger from being realized. The following exercise will help you do this.

Anger Exercise–Using your dominant hand write in the first column, "I am angry." In column two, using your least dominant hand, write your immediate response. *See the example below.* Going back and forth with these statements will dislodge the self-talk that represents your inner child's old belief systems. It will also flush out the responses that perhaps you as an adult have adopted as a way to continue the denial of these feelings.

The purpose of this exercise is to continue writing in the columns until you can righteously own the anger of your inner child. That way when you do your tapping the energy of that anger will be sufficiently stimulated in the electrical circuitry of your body to be neutralized. So try to continue until you can write, I am Angry," in both columns with no resistance.

EXAMPLE:

1. I am angry.	1. But they did the best they could.
2. I am angry.	2. But it's not her fault she died.
3.	3.
4.	4.
5.	5.
6.	6.
7.	7.
8.	8.
9.	9.
10. "I AM ANGRY!	10. "I AM ANGRY!"

Once done, bundle the baggage of your anger. I usually just draw the bag over the columns as a way of throwing them in one big bag. Then have your list in front of you when you do this round of tapping. Your psyche will automatically neutralize the anger on all levels available. You will also be able to use what you have written as your reminder phrases. You can do the few rounds I have provided, but then please tap using your own words. It will make your experience much richer.

EFT For Anger

"Even though I feel rage (anger, revenge, etc.) that I was left alone and felt so afraid, I want to finally feel safe and protected by adult self; I want to trust that I can express these feelings and still be loved. Continue with tapping around the points saying your reminder phrase until you feel flat.)

"Even though I later felt righteous as an adolescent because it enabled me to survive, I now want to express this anger. I know it was an expression of my hurt. I know it was triggered by this current loss but felt so familiar to when I had no power and felt so alone. But I'm not alone now, and I want to trust enough to say what I felt and to speak my truth."

So even though I felt anger inside, but did not dare to express it for fear of retaliation when I was powerless and at risk, that was then not now. Now, I want to neutralize those feelings. I want to trust my adult self to keep me safe while I finally speak my truth, let it go of this pain and be able to trust enough to feel joy.

Neutralizing the Negative

Side of the eye: *All of this rage…*

Corner of the eye: *this anger and rage…*

Under the eye: *Really uncomfortable with these feelings of anger*

Upper lip: *But felt so abandoned and alone, so violated and betrayed*

Lower lip: *It felt unsafe and wrong to feel this much rage.*

Collarbone: *It was not okay to feel such anger.*

Under the arm: *So I stuffed and pushed it back down......*

Chest bone: *But now it won't be pushed back down...*

Rib: *Even though it is so uncomfortable...*

Wrist:... *it won't go away...*

Head: *All of this anger... can't silence that voice... it's too late.*

Moving from the Possibility of Change to Conviction...

Side of the eye: *So maybe I can tap it away...*

Corner of the eye: *Give myself permission to speak my truth...*

Under the eye: *Speak my truth while I tap with my adult...*

Upper lip: *It sure has not worked to push it down...*

Lower lip: *I need to figure out a new way...*

Collarbone: *Perhaps if I tap while I vent...*

Under the arm: *I will finally be able to speak my truth...*

Chest bone:... *with the protection of my adult self...*

Rib: *Somewhere in time, this truth needs to be stated and heard*

Wrist: *If not now, when?*

Head: *If not with my adult self, then who else can I trust, where else can I turn?*

The inner Child finally speaks his or her truth!

Side of the eye: *I am angry!!!!*

Corner of the eye: *I didn't deserve what I got.*

Under the eye: *I deserved to feel loved.*

Lower lip: *I deserved to feel safe.*

Collarbone: *It was them not me!*

Under the arm: *I am no longer willing to take the blame...*

Chest bone:... *to feel shame about the person I am!*

Rib: *I am lovable!*

Wrist: *I did not deserve what I got...*

Head: *I can finally say that out loud and trust my words will be heard, and I will still be loved!*

Again, customize these statements and keep tapping on the end points until the anger is released and the inner child finally feels he or she has been heard and is still loved. Only then can the two of you, inner child and adult self, be free to move into the emptiness of the loss and, once and for all, acknowledge the void so it can be filled with love and light.

However, if there is still an edge to your anger, the following exercises will serve to rid your body of the energy. Some of these exercises are aimed at dislodging the inner child's anger. Some are simply to move the energy out of your body so you can let it go.

ADDITIONAL METHODS TO RELEASE YOUR ANGER

Pick and choose which methods appeal to you, but I do recommend that you always begin with the first one. Sealing your anger before you release it is just the responsible thing to do. Otherwise, the disruptive energy spews out in the universe and coagulates with other vibrational rage as well. This is why some are reluctant to express the anger–they do not want to put that energy out into the world. But if you take responsibility for working with it in a transformative way this does not happen. It is just energy that is recycled and transmuted for another higher use. So again, I recommend you always begin with creating protection around you and the release of your anger.

1. *Creating Protection*–First so that you and your inner child can always feel safe close your eyes and imagine that you surround yourself in that bubble light. Sometimes I call in an Angel or a Master or Loved one to assist. The, ask that your anger is encased in this light and that as you express it the anger be transmuted in violet light then be sent directly sent to the great central sun to be transformed. This will seal your anger so that its energy does not bleed out into other areas. When

you feel complete and secure proceed with any or all of the following exercises.

2. *The Silent Scream*–aka *Whisper Yelling*–*To* do this you can take a pillow and simply scream in it. Scream by opening your mouth but blocking the volume from coming out. It releases the frustration without alarming anyone around you.

3. *The Private Scream*–If you really need to release the volume of your anger then this method is an option. Scream in a car or in the woods where you will not be heard.

4. *Throwing a tantrum*–This is a wonderful exercise or activity that enables you to jump up and down, flailing your arms around and making grunting noises, or yelling "No," to what you are releasing and then ultimately yelling "Yes," to what you are want to attract. This resets the central nervous system immediately. Animals do this naturally when they have been stressed by a life-threatening experience.

5. *Exercising*–This releases the energy and makes it more manageable. (Note: aerobic exercise, such as jogging, etc. reduces current anger, anaerobic exercise, such as yoga, swimming, etc. reaches anger that is more deeply rooted in the muscular fibers.)

6. *Meditation*–Using the breathing techniques you were introduced to in the last section relax and go into a meditative state. Then invite your inner child into your mind's eye and listen to your inner child's anger. Allow it; you do not have to change it or fix it. You just have to help him or her discharge it responsibly so it does not bleed into inappropriate acting out in day-to-day life. This is useful if the tapping did not quite address the depth of your inner child's rage. You can tap as you hold this image in your mind's eye as well. That combination augments this method even more.

7. *Journal Writing*–I recommend when you record your responses in a journal that you use it for stream-of-consciousness

writing, recording without censure whatever thoughts and feelings come to mind. By the time you have finished your inner work, you will have a rich collection of the feelings you identified, experienced, resolved, and healed. It will be similar to having a photo album that documents your inner journey.

8. *Verbal and Written Dialogues*-Dialoguing is a tool that involves talking to the different parts within you; orchestrating an interaction so that a healing can occur. It can be done verbally, when you are actually stating the feelings of the different parts involved in the exercise, or it can be done by writing the responses of each character. When you are dialoguing between the adult self and a younger inner child, I suggest you use your least dominant hand to write your inner child's responses. It was difficult, as a child, to master the skill of writing. Sentences were shorter, words more direct. By using your least dominant hand, you will find that this experience is recreated. The more mature response of the adult self is experienced by using the hand you are most accustomed to using. This is true when you are dialoguing with the inner child about his or her anger. Ask questions.

9. *Drawing*-Drawing your pain frees your creativity and lets you give form to the feelings and the different internal characters without using words. Describing the voice of the critical self with words can be limiting; drawing often gives you a richer symbolic means of expression.

10. *Mirror Work*-Mirror work involves sitting in front of a mirror and having a dialog with your younger selves in order to observe the body and facial movements that accompany these parts within. It allows you to see for yourself how your shoulders slump when you speak from your child self, or how you wince when you express your inner child's fear. It also helps you see more clearly your physical demeanor from your adult point of view. Looking at yourself in a mirror is also one of the most effective ways of finding that higher, more evolved part of yourself. By facing yourself eye to eye, you can

look beyond your physical deficiencies and see the wise, inner being within you.

Once you feel the energetic shift of this younger one within you, and you can sense he or she has let go, you are ready to move on to the next stage.

STAGE FOUR - DESPAIR

When our inner child has finally been allowed to speak the truth, he or she collapses into the arms of the adult self in complete exhaustion. The truth has been acknowledged and contained. The despair in childhood was masked by shyness, lethargy, fear to engage, often mistaken for "quietness." But usually, that quietness was a loss of trust and a fear of retaliation if the true self was revealed. To truly embrace the source of our loss at such a young age would have put us at too much risk… the risk of not surviving the fear… risk of being exposed and punished… the risk of being shamed, blamed or humiliated.

So the despair for the inner child is more of an expression of the loneliness and the abandonment he or she felt at having to be so cut off from what was really felt. It was in response to the loss of the real self. As you saw in the overview of childhood grief, this stage of grief touches the loss of the real self, the angst felt in having to compromise the person we were in order to strive for the safety we needed to survive. The antidote for this despair is the adult self being able to assure the inner child that you have indeed evolved to a place where this is no longer true. It is welcoming the inner child back to his or her true essence, accepting him or her for the unique individual he or she truly is. It is done by validating the inner child's truth as was done in stage three and now allowing the inner child to tolerate the loss with your support.

EXERCISES FOR EXPERIENCING AND RELEASING YOUR DESPAIR

1. Write a letter to the younger parts of you who have had to let go. Welcome them into your force field, into a relationship with your higher guidance and the part of you who can tolerate this loss. This letter serves as a way to gather those parts of you that had to be sacrificed and banished in order for the inner child to survive. Acknowledging them by assuring their feelings will be heard, their needs met, makes this release more complete.

2. Take another piece of paper, write a second letter and let the inner child speak. Again, use your least dominant hand so the true feelings of that younger self can bypass the conscious mind and speak with more honesty and truth.

NOW WRITE DOWN ALL OF YOUR WORDS, PHRASES, AND PICTURES THAT CAPTURE THE DESPAIR OF YOUR INNER CHILD. LET HIM OR HER DRAW THE SADNESS AND EMPITNESS–THEN THROW ALL THAT YOU WANT NEUTRALIZE INTO YOUR BAG AND BUNDLE THE DESPAIR SO YOU CAN HELP OUR INNER CHILD LET IT GO.

EFT For Your Inner Child's Despair

"Even though I felt so much sadness, despair, and hopeless back I know it is now safe to let it go."

"Even though this sadness has felt as though it were more than I can bear, it feels so good to finally acknowledge the truth, to be honest with my adult self, so together we can begin to heal.

"So even though this truth has been buried for a very long time, it feels so relieving to lance this wound, to trust my adult self enough to open that door so ultimately we can begin to heal."

Continue with tapping around the end points saying your reminder phrases until you feel flat.

Neutralizing the Negative
Side of the eye: *So much sadness…*

Corner of the eye: *Have tried to run from it but failed…*

Under the eye: *Not sure how to feel…*

Upper lip: *I have cut off from this truth for so long…*

Lower lip: *The sadness, the despair, the emptiness, is so big…*

Collarbone: *Never thought I would be able to move beyond it and really heal?*

Under the arm: *Thought I was so alone like I would not survive?*

Chest bone: *It was so hard to tolerate that much emptiness…*

Rib: *No wonder I did not feel safe.*

Wrist: *That loneliness is almost more than I can bear.*

Head: *Can barely believe I survived.*

Moving from the Possibility of Change to Conviction…

Side of the eye: *But I am not alone, not like before.*

Corner of the eye: *I do have a support system…*

Under the eye: *I am getting stronger. I do trust my adult self and know he or she can help me let go.*

Upper lip: *I want to trust all of the resources he or she has gathered along the way.*

Lower lip: *My adult self has done a lot of work since then…*

Collarbone:… *there's a lot to offer that can help me heal.*

Under the arm: *Together we can neutralize the pain. I can feel safe enough to stand in the pain… I will not be standing alone.*

Chest bone: *We have come a very long way on this journey…*

Rib: *I am not alone… This is now, not then.*

Wrist: *I can release and let go.*

Head: *It truly is time to let go, to let God handle this so that we can heal.*

The Inner Child's Truth about the Despair!

1. *Go into a meditation and invite your inner child to write his or her pain of the void. Do so with your least dominant hand so the true essence of that younger self can emerge.*

2. *Then picture yourself as the adult holding the inner child in your arms or having your inner child sit near you enough to feel safe. Quiet yourself and be present enough to support this vulnerable one's admission of how alone he or she really felt.*

3. *Tap on your end points while you are listening. If that is too cumbersome invite your inner child to write down the truth of the despair, then imagine he or she reads it as you tap and neutralize the deeper levels of the pain.*

Keep tapping until you really feel the energetic shift of releasing and letting go. Customize your own reminder phrases so you can address the unique way you may experience this stage of grief.

Stage Five – Acceptance And Resolution

Acceptance and resolution of our loss mean that we have processed the first four stages of grief. We have addressed the residue of our essential wound–this loss triggered in our inner child–loss felt when as a child we felt powerless and feared we would not survive. All of that grief has now been resolved and released.

The following tapping sequence will anchor this new reality into your force field and that of your inner child as well. The meditation that follows is a wonderful way to wrap up the final stage of grief. With your inner child in your arms, you can now proceed on the journey of exploring the different realms of consciousness that enable you to pierce the veil between your physical world and the world of the unseen. But perhaps just as important you are now equipped to live your life with feelings, non-addictively, with the confidence that there is nothing with which you cannot cope. Your trust in self is an asset that not only benefits you it benefits all those in the world and actually humanity itself.

EFT For Acceptance And Resolution

Begin by tapping on the karate point for the setup statements. Then continue by tapping on each of the endpoints. This will anchor in this positive affirmation. Again, keep doing tapping rounds until you feel the "buzz." Hold the energy of this affirmation for 17 seconds as it takes form; then for another 68 seconds so your DNA can begin to replicate thus new picture and attract its vibrational match.

"Even though my inner child's grief got triggered in response to my recent loss, and he or she held this memory of not being safe, we have been reunited in trust and love. It IS safe to release all cellular memory of our grief, both present and past alike. We CAN now rewrite that cellular memory. With confidence, we know that we are loved by our Higher Source (God, Higher Power, etc.) enough to feel safe and to recommit.

So even though it has taken us a while to make peace, I am so grateful we navigated through this grief. I have finally found my way home, have reunited with my inner child, and am now ready to live life beyond fear knowing I will be able to cope.

So even though this has been a long time coming, we have finally healed enough to allow ourselves to expand and attract.

Continue with tapping around the points saying your reminder phrase until you feel flat or neutral.

Neutralizing the Residue of the Negative

Side of the eye: *This has taken a very long time.*

Corner of the eye: *Sometimes it felt as though I would never find the strength!*

Under the eye: *So many months for me......*

Upper lip: *And years for my inner child!*

Lower lip: *Wish I could have healed before... and not wasted so much time.*

Collarbone: *I wish we could have embarked on this journey before*

Under the arm: *Really wish I could have found peace at an earlier time.*

Chest bone: *Wish it had not taken the loss of my loved one...*

Rib:... *But I can now envision another level to this situation...*

Wrist: *And truth is I needed the current loss to flush out the old wounds*

Head: *That wounded one really needed to be healed.*

Moving from the Possibility of Change to Conviction...

Side of the eye: *I really could not know what I did not know...*

Corner of the eye: *Each stage of grief was valid in its own way...*

Under the eye: *I would not have had the compassion any earlier...*

Upper lip: *and without compassion, I could not have healed my inner child.*

Lower lip: *I want to focus on the fact that the time has finally come...*

Collarbone: *I could not know what I did not know...*

Under the arm: *I did the best I could with the resources I had at the time.*

Chest bone: *I am just glad the time has finally arrived...*

Rib: *We are now united, and the healing is done.*

Wrist: *My inner child and I are finally ready to move on.*

Head: *We are united, have let go and I can now expand.*

The last task of grieving involves forgiveness. What are you forgiving? Everything! You are ceremonialzing your forgiveness of your loved one for leaving you. Your inner child forgives you for taking so long to rescue him or her. Perhaps your inner child even forgives those who wronged him or her. And you forgive your higher guidance understanding you were not a victim of this loss. And last but not least you are asking your body to forgive you for bearing the brunt of your unresolved feelings and stress until you were truly ready to do for yourself what your body had been doing for you all these years.

The Hawaiian Forgiveness Ritual was given to me by a Hawaiian Elder named Josie. It is but one way to orchestrate a formal forgiveness. The shorter version is more popular and is included below. But I like to use this longer version when I am sealing a piece of work around grief. I use the shorter version for dissolving stress at the moment. Please feel free to use or create your own as well.

HAWAIIAN FORGIVENESS RITUAL – HO' OPONOPONO

Simply put, Ho'oponopono is based on the knowledge that anything that happens to you or that you perceive, the entire world where you live is your own creation and thus, it is entirely your responsibility–a hundred percent, no exceptions. Your boss is a tyrant. It's your responsibility. Your children are not good students. It's your responsibility.

There are wars and you feeling bad because you are a good person, a pacifist? The war is your responsibility. You see that children around the world are hungry and malnourished if not starving? Their want is your responsibility. No exceptions. The world is your world. It is your creation. As Dr. Hew Len points out– "Didn't you notice that whenever you experience a problem, you are there?"

It's your responsibility doesn't mean it's your fault, it means that you are responsible for healing yourself to heal whatever or whoever it is that appears to you as a problem.

It might sound crazy or just plain metaphorical, that the world is your creation. But if you look carefully, you will realize that whatever you call the world and perceive as the world is your world, it is the projection of your own mind. If you go to a party you can see how in the same place, with the same light, the same people, the same food, drink, music and atmosphere, some will enjoy themselves while others will be bored, some will be over enthusiastic and some depressed, some will be talkative, and others will be silent. The "out there" for every one of them seems the same, but if one was to connect their brains to machines immediately, it would show how different areas of the brain would come alive, how different perceptions there are from one person to the next. So even if they apparently share it, the "out there" is not the same for them, let alone their inner world, their emotions.

How do you heal yourself with Ho'oponopono? Three steps: by recognizing that whatever comes to you is your creation, the outcome of bad memories buried in your mind; by regretting whatever errors of body, speech, and mind caused those bad memories, and by requesting Divine Intelligence within yourself to release those memories, to set you free. Then, of course, you say thank You.

The long version… I recite this while tapping on the end points. It augments the clearing and neutralizes anything I might be holding onto in the unconscious.

FORGIVE ME_______________________________________

If I have hurt you

In any way, shape or form,

In thought, word or deed,

In any time, any place,

past, present or future

FORGIVE ME.

AND I, _____________________ FORGIVE YOU

For hurting me

In any way, shape or form,

In thought, word or deed,

In any time, any place,

Past, present or future

I FORGIVE YOU!

AND MAY THE CREATOR OF ALL THINGS FORGIVE US BOTH: ALL HO'OPONOPONO

IT IS DONE… SO BE IT!

This prayer can be said between you and another, between you and your body, between you and your inner child, between your Spirit and your Personality. It can be said to the one you have lost as a way to resolving their passing and a way to release the attachment so you both can move on.

The shorter, more popular version is simply:
I'm Sorry… Please Forgive Me
I love You… Thank You.

I repeat this over and over while tapping on my end points. Another one-liner I use to reduce the stress and anxiety before it even gets to stages two, three and four, is, **"God' love resolves this situation, (these feelings of loss) here and now."** Again, I say that repeatedly until the gut-wrenching feelings of loss subside.

This sequence can guide you through the progression.

The loss of your loved one has been acknowledged, processed, and released. The residual grief triggered in our childhood has been addressed. All resistance to expanding to the vibration where we can meet our loved one who has gone to the other side is now neutralized, and you can now choose to expand and begin the journey of your expanded relationship to your love that is not really gone.

You have also learned how to relate to your fragile one in a new and more profound way. Being able to embrace those parts within you that feel more vulnerable ensures that you will be able to respond to your fears instead of collapse and react from them.

In this next section I introduce you to my signature Seven Layer Healing Process. The sequential layers evolved in response to a personal healing session I did with of my inner seventeen year old. The Seven Layer Process was featured in my Share the Gift series which was developed in 2009. I offer it here just as an introduction.

It is particularly relevant to Beyond compassion because it really speaks to my personal experience of my essential wound… you will see how that wound haunted me for many decades and flavored not only my personal life choices but the choices I made for my career as well.

To further your work with your inner child I would suggest you explore my "Share The Gift" book and eBook modules which can be obtained on my website which again is www.EFTForYourInnerChild.com This model is fully explained in that series. It addresses the inner child sabotage from a spiritual perspective and targets four major issues of concern: attracting intimate relationships, abundance, right livelihood and reciprocal partnerships. The following overview will give you a bird's eye view of the process.

SECTION FIVE:
Cathryn's Signature Seven Layer Healing Process

MY INSPIRATION FOR THE BIRTH OF THIS MODEL

(Like most things, the "mother of intervention" is need. This model is no exception. Below is a letter that was written and emailed to the founder of EFT, Gary Craig, on 11/17/06. It was written after my first organic experience with what has now become the foundation for the merger of my inner child expertise with the innovative techniques of the new energy therapy called EFT.)

Dear Gary,

I just had the most profound experience with EFT. My name is Cathryn Taylor; I am the author of The Inner Child Workbook. My book has been out since 1991 and is considered one of the classics in the "inner child" field. For the past twenty years, I have been working with this concept and instructing others on how to identify and resolve their inner child's conflicts. Several years ago I came across your EFT techniques. Since then I have been applying them to addictive behaviors and teaching clients how to use them to mitigate their anxieties.

But today was a real milestone.

For the past several months, I have been facilitating "Teaching Your Inner Child the Law of Attraction", a new series that was inspired by the movie, "The Secret." As is usually the case, we teach what we need to learn. When we attract more Light, we illuminate that which vibrates at a lower frequency. The very act of teaching this subject uncovered my last cherished saboteur™ (my coined phrase for the part of us whose actions are intended to keep us safe, but whose impact keeps us from getting what we want).

"She" had been acting up ever since I taught my first class. This little one is my inner 17-year-old that is stuck in a moment of time when just as she was ready to leave for college, my father (her hero) had a nervous breakdown. That part of me has been held captive at that moment and has remained frozen ever since. According to the belief system of my inner adolescent, it became apparent today that any time I truly wanted to step into my mastery that would require "leaving" my father, this inner part of me would take hold of the situation. This inner 17-year-old would overeat and numb out my passion, thus sabotaging me along the way. No matter how healthy I got in all areas of my life, there was always the shadow part of me that maintained her loyalty to her father while silently lingering in a state of despair.

Today is the day that I finally put it all together. By teaching this inner adolescent how to do EFT, I brought her into my mind's eye and invited her not only to learn the principles of "The Secret," but to also learn how to cope with her despair and grief over dad's breakdown. I had used EFT to deal with emotional disturbances, but I had never considered going back in time through meditation to actually teach that frozen part of me how to tackle the gut-wrenching emotions of helplessness, fear, anger, embarrassment, and utter despair. That part of me was never able to cope with the fact that she could not save her father from his emotional demise. His breakdown had somehow become her failure and that failure translated into her not being able to fully succeed. It is amazing to me how a part of us can stay so incredibly loyal to the parent who does not cope with his or her own life. Afraid to surpass and abandon that parent, many of us sustain one area of our lives that remains dysfunctional.

Inner Child Work is based on externalizing the old wound, giving it a face, and then interacting with that part to make it feel safe. The model is a magical way of empowering our most competent adult selves while simultaneously being able to acknowledge and respond to our more frightened parts. It is a way to "repairent" ourselves. It is a way to "right" old wrongs… to retrain the brain to expect something new, healthy and life-giving. But today a miraculous shift occurred when I actually stepped back in time and taught my inner teen how to neutralize the frightening feelings of the time. Using EFT and guided inner child mediation I was able to go back to that frozen moment in Math class when she looked at the clock and knew at that exact moment her father, her hero, was getting electric shock treatment to eradicate his pain. Having identified with him to such a degree she wondered how long it would be before the same would be necessary for her. How could she deal with life any differently, she wondered?

I had been running from that moment and that question ever since. But today I was finally able to help her feel relief. Today I was able to set her, as well as myself, free. Faith was restored, and I am now able to step into the mastery I have worked so hard to achieve. I had done many meditations, but nothing had completed dissolved or neutralized the pain of that moment. This combination finally did just that. EFT is a brilliant method to neutralize the pain of our inner child's past. Thank you for bringing it to the world and for being so dedicated to teaching others how to use this tool to heal.

CATHRYN TAYLOR, MA, MFT, LADC

This particular experience inspired me to officially integrate EFT into my inner child work. What evolved was my specialized method of tapping I call *"Interactive Tapping".*™ It then became the foundation for my signature, *"Seven Layer Healing Process."*

BRINGING IT ALL TOGETHER

Combining the context of the inner child with the energetic interventions of EFT provides you with perhaps one of the most empowering avenues for working with those parts within you that sabotage your best efforts to succeed. Keep in mind that it is not the intention of our wounded ones to hold us back. Their efforts are merely aimed at sustaining a sense of safety; they do not realize that their actions sabotage the inner adult's success. They are frightened and are responding in the knee-jerk manner they developed in response to the original wound. It is the only way they know how to attempt to stay safe. When you empower your adult self, you provide these wounded ones with someone who can respond. You will then discover you have a wealth of energy that you can redirect and thus give birth to your ever-evolving future self.

The following progression of the layered Inner Child/EFT sequences offers you a method to step into the vibration of a healthy adult self. The sequences assist you in becoming empowered and coming into alignment with your wounded inner child that strongly holds on to that which keeps it safe. You then are able to heal and befriend this wounded one, so it can merge with you and experience joy. In order to regain his/her trust and thus heal, you must have a part of you that can respond in a nurturing and healthy manner and that can orchestrate a sequential progress. You must come into this interaction with an empowered adult who can respond in a compassionate manner. Why? Because if you begin digging into your past with no fresh methods for responding to that pain, you simply pull off the band-aid on an old wound while offering no hope of healing it.

The healing agent for an old wound is the interaction between the wounded one and an inner adult that can respond with compassion, love, and care.

This interaction changes the experience of the inner child and creates its reality. Remember that our mind does not know the difference between what is real and imagined. Just as we program our future with intentions and pretense exercises, we can do the same thing by returning to the time of the wound and changing the experience of the part of us that holds on to the pain.

Again, the only reason this is possible is because we have attained the level of empowerment that enables us, as adults, to intervene. We step into the original scene of the wound; on behalf of the inner child—we protect, retrieve, and rescue him/her from the hurtful experience.

If you think about it, it stands to reason that as we set our intentions for our heart's desires, we flush out the trailers that sabotage our efforts to succeed. When we attract more light, we also illuminate our shadow self and the wounded parts that inadvertently sabotage our efforts to succeed. But we can repair that wound and invite that essence back into the vibration of our force field where it can be safe if we give a face to those saboteurs that run rampant with their negative statements and destructive behaviors; if we learn how to relate to those wounded ones with care and love. Not only does this halt the sabotage, but it also augments the magic with which we can manifest.

Bring a child's imagination and wonderment into any intention, and the vibrational frequency increases tenfold.

THE SEVEN LAYERS OF HEALING

The following section describes the seven layers of healing featured in my newly developed Seven Layers Inner Child/EFT Sequence Procedure. This process systematically enables you, as the adult, to help the inner child heal, so it can also learn and experience the magic of the law of attraction. Each layer uses EFT sequences to accomplish the task stated. Because this process takes you through a step-by-step process, each layer respectively uses the pronouns appropriate to the task at hand. You 1) identify the contrasting feelings; 2) separate from and externalize that feeling so, as the adult, you can 3) respond to and, therefore, heal the contrasting emotion by relating to the feeling as an emotional expression of the child within that is afraid.

The following is a brief introduction to these respective layers. In Section Two, these layers are applied to the core issue of this e-Course. The youtube video links are taken from my 62-day upload that gives you an overview. I am including them here because they will give you a fuller experience of these layers. Please ignore any references to my blog – any information you need is included in this e-book.

1st Layer: Empowering and Clearing the Adult Self

This sequence neutralizes all disturbances currently being experienced in our day-to-day life. The stress we felt yesterday with respect to this topic is where we start. We use the pronoun

"i " to own any disturbance that is housed in the force field of our adult self.

2nd Layer: The Separation Step

When we separate from the part within us that experiences the disturbance, we externalize the disturbance and set up a dyad between the part of us that carries the wound and the part of us that can respond to the wound. This is a crucial step because this separation allows us to interact; the interaction between the wounded one and the healer within us creates the ultimate healing. We use the pronoun "he/she" to begin the separation process.

3rd Layer: The Interactive Step

We use the pronoun "you" to begin the interactive process. It is building a trusting relationship between our most illuminate/nurturing self and the wounded inner child/soul shadow. We are now doing a form of surrogate tapping (tapping on behalf of another). This creates the internal experience for the wounded aspect that finally someone is responding to his/her pain and is operating on his/her behalf. (This is true irrespective of the dimension of time or consciousness, be it an inner child or an aspect of your Soul. It is all a form of time travel anyway.)

The result, however, is that this interaction introduces the wounded one to the experience of deservedness and nourishes a sense of importance. Having the inner adult operate on its behalf invites this part to feel worthy of attention and care. This is an important step in the process of building trust because often the inner child has felt abandoned and left to fend for itself. This is true for aspects of your soul as well. They sustain a state of suspension waiting to be discovered, rescued, and healed. When we travel back in time to respond to their situation and to heal their pain, they are finally free to return to the light.

4TH LAYER: THE TEACHING STEP

Now, we shift into a meditative state and begin to teach our wounded inner child the technique for this neutralization process. In our mind's eye, we imagine we return to the scene of the wound. We go through a meditation that invites our wounded one to show us his/her pain. Together, you and your wounded one determine what needs to be healed, and you then assist this little one in tapping through his/her pain. You use the pronoun "I", but it is now being said from the experience of your wounded one. You are merely asking him/her to repeat, follow along, and experience how this technique can heal the antiquated pain.

5TH LAYER: THE MERGER STEP

This layer is used predominantly for the inner child only. With aspects of your soul, you want to simply escort them back into the light, so their energy can be freed. But with an aspect of your personality from this lifetime, you want to partner with him/her and build a bonding, cooperative relationship. Combining the neutralization process with the personal pronoun, we enables you to set up the merger and integration. Partnering with the inner child in this manner empowers him/her to return to your force field in a healed state. It enables you and your inner child to reclaim the magic that was lost while experiencing the wound. When you bring this magic back, the essence of the believability you have as a child returns as well. If you then infuse your manifestation with this vibration, you create magic tenfold!

6TH LAYER: REPROGRAMMING YOUR DNA; GIVING BIRTH TO A FUTURE SELF

This next sequence neutralizes any disturbance that your body has held on your behalf. In all dimensions of time and consciousness, this sequence restores your DNA to the recalibrated vibration that can now hold your new alignment and intention. This process gives substance to who you want to become. You first clear the disturbance from your body by asking for its forgiveness, give it permission to release, and infuse it with the vibration of the new you. This reprograms the DNA in every cell to hold your new vibration. A meditation, specific to this purpose, guides you through this process.

7TH LAYER: GLOBAL STEP

Using EFT, this final sequence takes all you have neutralized and realigned; it then sends this energy into the Universe as an offering for planetary healing. It reinforces the fact that you are part of something bigger than yourself. You are a valuable agent of change for mankind.

Again, if you are interested in pursuing your inner child work please check out the Share the Gift Book and 4 part module eBook Series which can be found on my website.